THE TOUR

THE TOUR

········· A MEMOIR ··········

DENISE SCOTT

hardie grant books

MELBOURNE · LONDON

Published in 2012 by Hardie Grant Books

Hardie Grant Books (Australia)
Ground Floor, Building 1
658 Church Street
Richmond, Victoria 3121
www.hardiegrant.com.au

Hardie Grant Books (UK)
Dudley House, North Suite
34–35 Southampton Street
London WCZE 7HF
www.hardiegrant.co.uk

Cataloguing-in-Publication data is available from the National Library
of Australia.

The Tour
ISBN 978 1 74066 905 4

Cover design by Josh Durham/Design by Committee
Text design by Vivien Valk
Typesetting by Kirby Jones

Printed and bound in Australia by Griffin Press

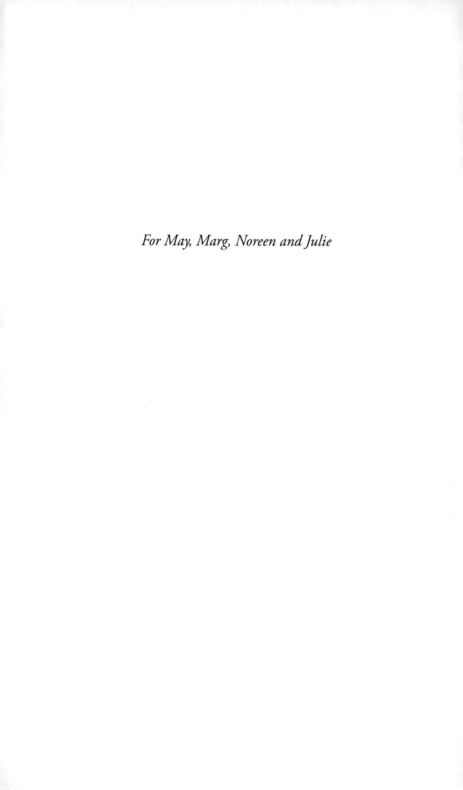

For May, Marg, Noreen and Julie

Contents

The awakening

It was the year 2009 and I was fifty-four years old and it was the night before I was due to go away on a tour and I drank too much.

When I say I drank too much, allow me to be specific. I shared a bottle of wine with my partner, John, but then suspecting he might have had a bit more than me I went to open a second bottle so I could pour myself another glass.

Just as I reached for the second bottle, however, John said, 'Hang on, Scotty, do you have to open that one?'

Was the man insane?

'It's just that it's a really good bottle, and I was hoping to cellar it for a few years.'

What a wanker! Life's too short to wait for wine to age. Besides, we don't have a cellar.

(Here I must apologise to those who read my previous book, *All That Happened at Number 26*, not for the book—God knows, I did my best—but because I need to repeat a story. But I promise to make it as brief as possible. Then again, if you're anything like me you'll have no memory of it anyway.)

When I was four years old I was standing in my Nanna Scott's kitchen and she said, 'What do you want on your sandwich, Denise, Vegemite or peanut butter?' And then she dropped dead. Just like that. There she was, standing at the kitchen table as large as life one minute, and then, bingitty-bang, dead on the floor the next.

Well, I wasn't expecting it. And I'm pretty sure Nanna wasn't. A massive heart attack. She was fifty-nine years old.

I never had time to tell her, 'Vegemite, Nanna, Vegemite.'

My father met the exact same fate: fatal heart attack at fifty-nine. And since I'm now well into my fifties … You don't have to be Einstein to join the dots.

That was why, when John told me not to open that second bottle of wine, I responded, 'John, you know there's a history of people suddenly dropping dead in my family. That could be me tonight—standing talking to you one minute and then dead on the floor the next—and who would you drink your fancy bottle of wine with then? Your new floozy? The one you meet at my funeral?'

What could he say?

Triumphantly, I opened the bottle and poured myself a glass, or rather a goblet, or more precisely a small fish bowl— this probably best describes 'Mummy's bucket', as we like to call it at our house.

When I was almost finished John stood up and announced, 'I'm going to bed.'

'Oh, John, you don't want to have just one more tiny snifter of wine?'

'No. And I don't think you should either, Scotty. Remember what happened last year?'

Tragically, I did remember. And it wasn't pretty.

I was on another tour at the time, had drunk too much the night before and on the morning in question had to fly in a small plane. It was a bit turbulent, and when we landed one of the young boy comics asked if he could carry something for me. I said thank you and handed him my plastic bag of vomit, which I don't think he was expecting.

John put the cork back in the wine bottle, assuring me he was doing it for my own good. He put the bottle on the kitchen bench and both wine glasses into the dishwasher. He then headed to the bathroom.

I waited until I heard the sound of his electric toothbrush then got a clean wine glass out of the cupboard and, just in case John suddenly stopped cleaning his teeth, turned the tap on full bore to cover the *glug-glug-glugging* sound as I quickly poured myself some more wine. Only a quarter of a glass. Or maybe it was a half. Possibly it was verging on three-quarters. Whatever, let's not get bogged down in dreary details.

The reason I drank so much that night was that I was scared. And depressed. As I said to John later that night as we lay in bed, 'I don't want to go.'

'Why not?'

'I'm too old.'

'You are not.'

'I am, John. I'm too old to be going on a Comedy Festival Roadshow. Do you realise I'm older than all the other comedians' *mothers*?'

'Bullshit.'

'It's true.'

'What about Jeff Green? He's in his forties, isn't he? You can't be older than *his* mother.'

'I could. She could have had him when she was twelve. These things happen. Anyway, I'm not funny. At least, I'm not funny enough. They didn't even laugh at my finger-up-the-arse routine last night.'

'Scotty, it was a prostate cancer fundraiser. They were a bit sensitive, that's all. And they *did* laugh; you just couldn't hear them.'

'Why wouldn't I hear an audience laughing, John?'

'I don't know. It could have been the ceiling. You know, it was very high, and all the sound was probably getting sucked up into the roof before it reached you on the stage.'

The old sound-getting-sucked-up-into-the-ceiling routine. John might as well have got a knife, stuck it in my heart and slowly twisted it.

'Oh John …' I moaned, indicating extreme emotional pain, 'of all the places we could go we're touring to Far North Queensland.'

John said nothing. It was almost as though he didn't understand the significance of this statement. I had to up the ante.

'Far North fucking Queensland, John!'

It worked. John responded, although I noted he sounded tired. 'The problem being?'

'The problem being I'm fat.'

'You're not that fat, Scotty.'

'What do you mean, not that fat? Fat is fat, John, and I'm fat. I mean, I wouldn't care if we were going to Tasmania …'

'What, do you think Tasmanians are more accepting of fat people or something?'

'No, John. I mean, if I was going to Tassie I wouldn't have to wear bathers. But Far North Queensland … Oh God, I should have had waxing done. You know how hairy I get. Jesus, these days I have to have a bikini wax not so I can wear bathers, but so I can wear knee-length shorts. And how am I going to explain why I have to wear a scarf in the tropics?'

'Why *do* you have to wear a scarf in the tropics?'

'Because, in case you haven't noticed, my neck is covered in goobies and skin tags and warts. And what am I going to do when the arthritis in my ankle gets so bad it seizes up and I can't walk and I just have to drag my leg along behind me? You won't be there to massage it, John. I mean, I can't ask one of the young boy comics, "Could you please rub my fat old lady's ankle?" And what about when we're all driving around in the mini-van together? What will I talk to those young boys about? Menopause? My dry vagina?'

'Well, gee, Scotty, if anything's going to get a young man to look up from his iPhone …'

I woke with a start. My mouth was dry. I picked up the orange Tupperware cup that sat on my bedside table and took a sip of water. I marvelled at its refreshing coolness. We were so lucky to live in Melbourne—such lovely water, so clear, so clean … Oh, Jesus, my head hurt. I groaned. Why had I drunk so much?

I hung over the side of the bed. Ouch. Upside down, my head thumped even more. I picked up the radio alarm clock and turned it to face me. The bright-green numerals informed me it was 2.06 am. This meant I had slept for approximately two hours. That was, more than likely, all the sleep I was going to get, because not only was I a hormonal woman in my fifties who had drunk too much but I was also a chronic insomniac.

I got up and went to the toilet. On my return journey I went via the kitchen and had a couple of Panadols.

Back in bed I made a distinct whimpering sound. Immediately, right on cue, John started stroking my head. Ten seconds later his breathing pattern indicated he was sound asleep again, as did the fact that his hand had become a dead weight on top of my face and I had to lift it off in order to breathe.

And so I lay there.

Worrying.

About everything.

I worried about John having an affair and falling in love and possibly even leaving me and having a baby with Ruth, one of his work colleagues. I mean, why wouldn't he? She was hot and, what was more, clearly loved the way he played his ukulele (and no, that isn't a euphemism). And hadn't she only a week earlier told John she loved his wild, silver hair? In fact, hadn't she told him he looked like Richard Gere? That was the same day I'd told John he looked mental and needed a haircut.

I worried about our kids. Of course I did. I had good reason. Our twenty-three-year-old-daughter, Bonnie, was a video installation artist! For God's sake, what the hell was a video installation artist? I didn't have a clue. All I did know was that she and her boyfriend had recently moved to Berlin, where they were surviving on a sack of potatoes and wine that cost fifty cents a litre. The day before departure she'd announced to John and me: 'You guys do understand what's going on here, don't you? I'm not just going travelling, you know. I'm going to Berlin to live. I might be gone forever.' Since I'd seen how much, or rather how little, Bonnie had in her bank account, I considered that highly unlikely.

But on the night before I went away on tour I was extremely focussed on one specific worry—namely that Bonnie had been murdered in a forest somewhere in Portugal. It wasn't out of the question; after all, at that moment in time she was in Portugal, and as far as I knew (although geography has never been my strong suit) they had forests there, and what's more, she was participating in a visual arts workshop run by a philosopher who wore a black skivvy! I may have made up the black skivvy bit, but whatever. He was a philosopher running a visual arts workshop! What mother wouldn't be having an anxiety attack? Bonnie had met him at a dinner party in Berlin. Apparently he was 'amazing,' and had offered her the workshop for free, assuring her he'd also find somewhere for her to sleep. I bet he will, was my immediate thought. Oh why did we ever lend her the money for the airfare? What idiots we'd been. Oh God. Oh please, please, please let her be okay. If only I could ring her. But that was out of the question because, as usual, she had no phone credit.

I worried about my twenty-five-year-old son, Jordie, being a drug addict. Why wouldn't he be? He was a musician! And there was that ex-girlfriend who'd posted on YouTube that song she'd written about him snorting coke for breakfast, morning tea, lunch, afternoon tea and dinner. According to her he even sprinkled it on his cornflakes! I'd got quite a shock when I first saw it. But my son had assured me, 'Mum, she's exaggerating.' And, when I thought about it, that was more than likely true. For starters, he didn't eat cornflakes, never had: he was allergic to milk.

I worried about why, at the age of fifty-four, I was continuing to torture myself in a quest to become a good stand-up comedian. It was a young person's game. I was at best mediocre, and nothing annoyed me more than a mediocre comic with half-arsed commitment. Oh God, the thought of walking out onstage and banging on about getting older, being a mum, being overweight, blah, blah, blah—it made me feel sick. It brought me no joy. I felt entirely shithouse about it. So why not quit comedy? Yes! That was what I'd do. At the end of the tour I'd quit comedy for good.

Insomnia makes you think crazy thoughts. And the worst part is that they go on and on and on because the night goes on and on and on.

At one point my chest tightened and I wondered if it was a heart attack. What if this was it? What if I died? At least I wouldn't have to go away on tour.

I closed my eyes and tried the old counting-sheep routine but became distracted wondering where the sheep went after they jumped over the stile; when they left my head, where did they go? Did they gambol and frolic in a nearby field or …? And that was when I saw a neon sign blinking the word 'abbatoir'. Not that I'm a vegetarian—I love a chop as much as the next person—but it was upsetting to realise that in the process of helping me get to sleep those innocent lambs were being sent to their deaths. But then again maybe it was just the same three sheep going around and around?

I sighed.

And, would you believe it, a couple of seconds later John woke up and said, 'What's the matter, Scotty?'

I find that sort of thing totally amazing. I guess it's what comes from being with someone for thirty years. All I'd had to do was sigh …

And then sigh again …

And again … making each sigh louder and more distressed until I was sort of crying, and then I started to toss and turn quite ferociously, throwing the doona off and on, at one point pausing to hurl the 'stupid fat fucking European pillow' across the room. 'Why do they exist? You can't sleep on them. And oh, that fucking streetlight.'

I actually said the words aloud. But the light was shining right into my face. Wasn't that why we'd had holland blinds custom-made in the first place—to stop the streetlight coming in? And what had happened? The blind man came, took the measurements, went away, made the blinds, came back, installed them, and that first night I was forced to wonder if the blind man wasn't indeed just that—blind as a bat—because the new blinds were too narrow and the light was still pouring in. And what did we do about it? Nothing. Absolutely nothing. Sure, John did ring the blind man the next morning and leave a message saying there was a problem and could he ring back asap, but that was sixteen years ago and we were still waiting for him to call.

And then, after moaning about the light, I leant over and whispered in John's ear, 'John? John? John, are you awake?'

And then with my index finger and thumb I got a teeny tiny bit of skin on his back and gently twisted it.

And then I sighed again.

And then, incredibly, John just woke up … intuitively.

'What's the matter, Scotty?'

'I can't sleep.'

'Come here.'

I shuffled backwards towards John and we lay spooning, one question mark inside another.

'Geez, you've got a great arse, Scotty.'

'Oh John …'

'You have. You've got a really great arse.'

'Yeah, okay, I've got a great arse. Whatever. I just wish I could sleep.'

'I know something that will help you to sleep.'

'Oh no, John, not now.'

It has to be said that John is the most optimistic human being I have ever met. In the most hopeless of circumstances he never gives up.

'I'll tell you a dirty story.'

'John, please, no.'

And away he went. 'Okay, I'm home alone in bed when suddenly I wake up and I see a woman. It's you, Scotty.'

'Good call, John.'

'You walk into my room. You're wearing a see-through dress and you've got nothing on underneath.'

'I've changed my mind. I don't want to be in your story. I don't want to be naked in a see-through dress.'

'Why not?'

'Because these days I can't get away without at least wearing a bra and underpants.'

'But Scotty, you look beautiful.'

'In *your* head I look beautiful, but in *my* head I look disgusting, so please get me out of your story.'

'Well, okay then, I'm in bed and this beautiful woman with long dark hair walks in.'

'Long dark hair? Are you talking about Ruth?'

'Who the hell is Ruth?'

'Who the hell is Ruth? You know exactly who Ruth is.'

'I don't, Scotty.'

'Ruth is that spunky woman at your work who said you look like Richard Gere.'

'Oh, for God's sake.'

'Well, she's got long dark hair and she'd look hot in the nude.'

'I'm not talking about Ruth. I'll start again, okay? Alright. I'm in bed and this woman with short red hair ...'

'Julia Gillard?'

'Oh, Scotty ...'

'I don't mind if it is. For some reason I don't find that situation threatening.'

'Let's forget about hair. A woman walks into my bedroom. She's wearing a see-through dress. Slowly she unbuttons it and it slips to the floor. She gets into bed and curls around me. I feel two hard things pressing into my back. They feel like macadamia nuts.'

'Macadamia nuts?'

'Her nipples …'

'She's got nipples like macadamia nuts?'

'Yeah, I wasn't sure about the macadamia nuts either. What about pistachios? Shelled.'

'What?'

'The pistachios, they'd be shelled.'

Needless to say, nothing happened. Within a minute John was once more sound asleep.

I lay there and obsessed about what sort of nut would make a good nipple. Brazil? Cashew? Peanut? I moved on to dried fruit. The muscatel came close.

We'd just turned into Bell Street when I felt it. It was on my chin. What the hell? Hadn't I just done a thorough check for facial hairs before leaving the house?

Oh my godfathers. I felt another one. They must have grown since I'd got into the cab. Great. At this rate I'd have a full-on beard by the time I reached the airport.

'Oh no.'

I must have said the words aloud, because the taxi driver looked at me via the rear-vision mirror, a concerned expression on his face. 'Something wrong?'

'No, it's nothing. I just remembered I left something at home, that's all.'

'Wanna go back?'

'No, no, it'll be fine.'

Going all the way back home for a pair of tweezers seemed a little crazy, although if I hadn't known for certain I could buy some at the airport I sure as hell would have considered it.

At the airport I headed straight to the pharmacy and then to the ladies, where, with the aid of my el cheapo 2.5 spectacles, I did my plucking with the newly purchased tweezers. Then, with all the renewed confidence a hairless chin can bring a middle-aged woman, I headed to the departure lounge.

Gideon, the tour manager, was already there. He had Ray-Bans sitting on top of his head, expensive aqua-coloured trainers on his feet—which I couldn't help but think a brave choice—a tasteful small-checked designer suitcase in one hand and a disgusting oversized, putrid, filthy, bright-orange case in the other. He let go of the luggage and gave me a kiss on the cheek. 'Ms Scott, how are we?' He nodded his head towards the orange monstrosity. 'That's the merch. Coffee cups. Can you fucking believe it? We have to sell Comedy Festival coffee cups at the gigs. How funny is that?'

'Not very,' I replied, and we both laughed until we cried.

Next to arrive was Stu, the tech for the tour. He had longish dreadlocks casually pulled up into a high ponytail that bordered on being a bun. There was a pale-blue stud in his nostril and a silver ring in his brow. Gideon introduced us. We shook hands. He had a lovely warm, friendly smile.

A few minutes later Josh Earl arrived. Good God, that boy looked as though he'd just come out of the womb. How old was he? Surely no more than twelve.

He was followed by Jeff Green, who looked pretty damn good for a man in his forties, all rosy cheeked and pretty much wrinkle free. Yes, I thought to myself, I could easily be older than his mother.

Last to arrive, and quite breathless, were Russell and Sadie. (Lee, Benny and Jordan, the young trio known as Axis of Awesome, were flying out from Sydney and meeting up with us at Brisbane airport.) Russell Kane, a British comic, was the international act for our tour; Sadie was his fiancée. We Australians weren't allowed to take partners on the roadshow, but the internationals were able to do so. I guess it was the only way we could get them to stay in the colony.

I hadn't met Russell before. He was charming and energetic and, as it turned out, a brilliant comic. Audiences loved him. But it was Sadie who knocked me for six. She was quite possibly the most beautiful young woman I had ever seen: perfectly shaped pale-pink lips, vivid-green eyes, long dark lashes, shiny jet-black hair, high cheekbones, long legs, pert breasts and a fabulous cleavage that somehow gave the impression of being accidentally on show, as though Sadie had simply grabbed the first top she could find with no regard to the final effect. And what an effect. She had that head-turning movie-star quality you rarely ever see in the flesh. Sadie's skin was that smooth, creamy, white English skin and was utterly perfect, and what amazed me the most was the fact that this perfection was so evenly distributed. Her face, neck, cleavage, arms, legs: every part of her was smooth and creamy and white and even in tone. It was all I could do to stop myself from reaching out and touching her.

I rearranged my scarf, making sure my neck was covered, and wished I'd done something about the red, blotchy, sun-damaged skin on my forehead. What am I saying? I had done something! I had been to see a skin specialist who had suggested, 'You could always grow a fringe.' I had heeded his advice. But at that moment, as I stood in the airport lounge gazing upon the lovely Sadie, I realised a fringe wasn't enough.

There was no getting around it: I felt like shit.

I gave myself a mental pep talk. I told myself to get a grip and stop being ridiculous. Who the hell did I think I was, a young woman? Had I forgotten that we middle-aged women were invisible? (And to think some people see that as a negative. No way. Women becoming invisible is brilliant. Nobody notices your wrinkles, the extra weight, the grey hair, the thickening skin, because nobody notices you at all. They can't see you! I feel exactly the same about my deteriorating eyesight: it's fantastic—all the better not to see myself with.)

Sadie bent over and rummaged around in her enormous carry-on bag. She was wearing an extremely short, summery cotton skirt. She stood up and must have noticed me looking at her. How could she not? My mouth was hanging open. For that matter, so was everyone else's. Her hands flapped about apologetically. 'I know, my skirt, it's ridiculous. I shrank it in the clothes dryer last night. I'm such an idiot. I didn't know it had shrunk until I put it on this morning, and by that time the taxi was there to take us to the airport, and I'm looking through my case to find something else to wear, and then Russell's panicking, saying, "We're going to miss the plane!"

so I just thought, Bugger it, everyone can look at my arse, I don't care.'

Sadie, I thought, With an arse like that, why *would* you care?

I was the last one in our group to step up to the check-in counter. My heart was pounding and I felt sick. I had my reasons.

'Name?'

'Denise Scott.'

'Could I see some ID, please?'

'I haven't really got any,' I laughed.

The airline lady didn't laugh.

'Drivers licence?'

'I don't have one.'

'You don't have a drivers licence?'

She sounded as though she couldn't believe it.

(What was the big deal? Just because I was the only adult in the entire continent of Australia who didn't have one …)

'No, I don't.'

'That's okay; your passport will do.'

'I don't have one of those, either.'

'No passport?'

'It got stolen.'

'When did that happen?'

'Just last week.' (Or maybe it had happened six months ago, or, come to think of it, could it really have been over a year since I'd walked out of that cafe without it?)

'Have you reported it?'

'Of course.' I left the words 'I haven't' unspoken.

'Well, have you got any photo ID at all?'

I rummaged in my handbag. 'What about this?'

She looked at the plastic-covered card. 'What is this?'

'It's my Comedy Festival pass. You see that …' I pointed to a tiny photo in the top left-hand corner, half the size of a postage stamp. 'That's my head.'

'But what is it for?'

'It's what I used to get into the Comedy Festival club.'

She handed me my boarding pass. I smiled. She didn't.

When we arrived in Mackay we drove straight to the motel, a brown-brick two-storey building conveniently located 3 kilometres out of town. There was no hint that we were in tropical Far North Queensland until you looked up and there was sky, so much sky, and the smell—a delicious fragrance of frangipani mingled with Hungry Jack's, which, much to the delight of the Axis of Awesome boys, was located just across the road.

In the reception the manager handed us our room keys and asked for credit cards. I burnt with shame. 'Um, I don't have one. I usually just leave a cash deposit.'

'That'll be fine, but if I could just get some ID—your drivers licence, perhaps?'

Gideon stepped up to the counter and offered his credit card details on my behalf.

The manager then said, 'Unfortunately, we don't have wireless, so you'll need this to hook up to the internet.' He handed everyone a cable. I took one—easier than having to explain I hadn't brought my laptop. I had a laptop: John had given it to me the previous Christmas, and I loved it—used it every single day. But, as I'd explained to John earlier that morning, I couldn't take it away with me because—and it killed me to admit this—I'd never used it as a laptop before, as in I'd never taken it outside my office. Not once. 'I wouldn't know what to do, John.'

'They'll give you a password, and you type it in, and you'll be connected.'

'No I won't, John. It's never that simple with me. And what if I had to use one of those cable things? I don't even know where to plug them in.'

'It's easy. I'll show you.'

'But what about the other end? In the hotel room?'

'It'll be obvious, Scotty.'

'But what if it's not?'

'You'll be travelling with a group of young people. Ask them. They'd love to help you.'

But I couldn't do that. I would have felt like a fool. And so here I was in a motel room with no computer, and the weird thing was, that made me feel even more foolish.

The room was plain but functional: brown-brick walls, comfortable double bed, clean sheets, a small TV with an uncomplicated remote, some instant coffee, a box of longlife milk and two complimentary biscuits in cellophane packaging. It might have been a little soulless, but it was free of clutter, and as someone who hails from a house full of what I fondly like to call 'shit', where kitchen lights could be out of action for seven years before an electrician was called, I loved this motel room with its functioning fluorescent light.

I lay down on the bed and stared at the ceiling. What else was there to do? I had no computer. I thought about the fact that I also had no drivers licence, no passport and no credit card and was forced to ask myself if indeed I did exist. If so, given the circumstances, why didn't I just go the whole hog and pop on a floral frock and sun bonnet, get me a horse and gig, bake some bread and go and live with the Amish?

Because the Amish don't drink alcohol, that's why.

Later that afternoon we gathered in the foyer, where we were introduced to Jeremy, a journalist from the local paper. 'So how's the tour been going?'

'It's been brilliant, bloody brilliant,' Jeff answered.

'Where have you been so far?'

'Let's see.' Jeff rubbed his chin, appearing to ruminate. 'We've been to our motel rooms, which are very nice, and … that's about it, really.'

'And Hungry Jack's,' Jordan chipped in.

Jeremy introduced us to Stan, the photographer, who wanted to get a few 'whacky' shots to accompany the article, even though there was no article to be had. We obligingly climbed into a white Tarago and headed to the nearest location with a tropical feel.

I had never walked between rows of sugarcane before. None of us had. I thought about Roo and Barney and Pearl and Olive. I loved that play, *Summer of the Seventeenth Doll.* So this was where Roo and Barney worked. It was so green, like plush carpet. And the cane was so tall and thick on either side—it was like a jungle.

'Stop!' Stan the photographer yelled.

We turned around to face him.

'Okay, now GO!'

Dutifully, we held hands and skipped towards the camera, laughing our heads off, evoking the strong bond that being on the road together for less than a day can bring.

It killed me. The arthritis in my right ankle hurt like hell. But I said nothing. I even jumped when commanded—not easy with that wonky ankle and big breasts.

At 7.30 pm Gideon gathered us together backstage at the Mackay Entertainment & Convention Centre and told us the line-up for the show. In comedy there is a very straightforward approach to sorting out order of appearance: basically, you go in order of funniness. The least funny performer goes on first, and you proceed accordingly, working your way towards the final, headline act—the funniest.

'Okay, Denise, you're on first.'

Oh God, kill me. Kill me now. I felt sick. A tsunami of hopelessness threatened to engulf me. What the fuck was I doing? I'd been in the biz for twenty years and I was going on first?

I found a dressing room, a dull brown-brick cloakroom with a pale-yellow linoleum floor and Hollywood light globes surrounding the large mirror. I switched them on; only two lit up. If I had been asked to describe in one word what I was feeling at that moment I would have said, without any hesitation, 'Disappointed.' Disappointed with my face. Disappointed with my personality. Disappointed with my career. But, most of all, disappointed that I was disappointed.

I willed my spine to keep me upright, but it was no use. I physically slumped. Oh God, how much did I not want to go onto that stage? I forced myself to sit back up, and that was when I ascertained that the benchtop was made of a soft wood—my teeth marks were in it.

I began applying my new Laura Mercier make-up. It had cost a fortune, but, as the salesgirl in David Jones had said, 'It's worth it—such a smooth finish. If you were to wear anything heavier your face would just look dead.' I spread the foundation across my skin and then added concealer. Could concealer hide my age, my fear? I put on some mascara. I did another quick check for facial hairs. All clear.

I was already dressed in my stage outfit. I was wearing a pair of *miracle* jeans, the miracle being that they promised to make you look one size smaller, which they did for a whole minute, until all the fat that was being squashed down just went, 'Oh, fuck that,' and came splodging back out over the top of the waistband. It was the same with my minimiser bra: 16G promised to make me look 16F, but how was this possible? That extra breast fat had to go somewhere, and I'm here to tell you where: under your arms. It's true. Take it from someone who spent a whole day trying to put her arms down by her sides. I could not do it. I had perfect little A-cup breasts under my armpits and F-cup breasts out front.

However, I was pleased as punch with my top. It was a gorgeous silky, flowy, bluey-green sheer number that came perilously close to being a caftan without actually being one, a detail I found tremendously comforting. I was also happy with my necklace. Just as well: it had cost a small fortune. It was a heavy Moroccan-silver pendant in the shape of a heart, with fine gold-filigree detail. And to think I nearly hadn't bought it.

As I'd explained to the woman in the jewellery store, 'I love it, but I've already got a silver necklace at home.'

'Can I ask what it's like?' she had replied.

'It's a large butterfly —'

'Butterfly?'

'Yes, it's a butterfly, and —'

'Are its wings open?'

'Yes.'

The horrified look on the saleswoman's face indicated this was not the right answer. 'Denise, can I tell you something? Big-breasted women like yourself should never wear a butter-fly with open wings on their chest. A wide necklace makes your breasts look even bigger, whereas this necklace narrows down towards the cleavage and takes focus away from your breasts.'

I went and stood at the side of the stage. I peeked a look at the audience. I wished I hadn't. The average age appeared to be seventeen.

The lights went down in the auditorium. Chaser lights flashed around the edge of the stage. Edgy, loud contemporary music played as Jeff, the MC for the show, bounded on and grabbed the mike out of the stand. 'Hi, Mackay, how youse going? Are you ready for a big night?'

Judging by the screams from the crowd they were indeed ready for a big night.

I closed my eyes and concentrated on my breathing and my mantra: 'As soon as this tour finishes I can quit. As soon as this tour finishes I can quit. As soon as this tour finishes I can quit.'

Meanwhile, Jeff, as they say in the trade, was killing. The

audience loved him. 'But enough of me! It's time for the real funny stuff now, so, ladies and gentlemen, without further ado, make welcome our first act for this evening ...'

I took a deep breath. This was it. I wanted to vomit.

'This woman is one of the funniest women I know. She is a legend.'

Legend! God, how that word depressed me. Why not just say 'old' and be done with it?

'You may have seen her on the TV or heard her on the radio. You are going to love her, so go wild, go crazy, go absolutely mental, Mackay, and give it up for the one, the only, the hilarious ... MS DENISE SCOTT!'

Oh, that name. Denise Scott. Honestly, it had all the excitement of air escaping from a beach ball.

I walked onstage.

Twenty minutes later I walked off.

I'd gone okay. Quite good, in fact. Even my incontinence gag had worked. Not that it had been a straightforward triumph; indeed, at one point I'd appeared to be hurtling towards an almighty train wreck, quite possibly the biggest of my career, and that's really saying something.

It was a routine I'd done many times. As usual, I started by asking if there were any adult kids in the audience who still lived at home with their parents. Immediately, a girl way up at the back of the theatre raised her hand.

'And how old are you?' I asked.

'Thirty-seven,' she replied.

Thirty-seven and still living at home with her parents? I was rapt. This was comedy gold! I became so excited that I left the stage and headed into the audience, making my way to the back of the theatre, cracking jokes at this woman's expense the whole way. If I say so myself, the audience ate it up—they were killing themselves laughing.

Finally, I reached the woman in question. 'So you're thirty-seven years old and you still live at home with your parents. Why?'

'Denise,' she replied, 'the reason I still live with my parents is that I am intellectually disabled.'

Silence.

In fact, that night I learnt that there are many, many different levels of silence. And this was a very, very deep silence.

I had absolutely no idea what to say or do. And so I just stood there, and then I did something I have never done in my career, before or since. I hid behind a large pillar. It was situated on the right-hand side of the stage. What was I thinking? Obviously, I was going to have to come out at some point. I guess I was trying to give myself a bit of time out, hoping for some sort of miracle. A mini earthquake, perhaps? Anything that might distract from the reality of the situation.

I started whimpering into my handheld microphone, 'I don't know what to do. I don't know what to do …'

Then, from the back of the theatre, the thirty-seven-year-old woman called out, 'Don't worry, Denise. I still think you're funny.'

The audience laughed.

And as I emerged from behind the pillar and walked back to centre stage she added, 'But then again, I *am* intellectually disabled.'

And to think I'd almost stopped believing in miracles.

The next day our photo appeared in the paper. It was the group shot from the cane fields. Russell appeared to be leaping 2 metres in the air, his legs spread wide, his hands touching his toes. He was grinning his head off. I, on the other hand, appeared to be very much still on the ground, a pinched, wincing, almost bitter expression on my face. At the time I would have sworn I was smiling.

Maybe it was being in the tropics. Maybe it was being in the company of young people. Maybe it was being away from home, away from my day-to-day responsibilities. Whatever the reason, the fact was, the further north we went, the better I began to feel. I was lighter in spirit. (Ah, if only I could have been lighter in body as well.)

Nothing particularly noteworthy had happened in the two and a half weeks since we'd left Melbourne. Of course, there was that bowl of porridge I ate in Gladstone—if it wasn't the best I've ever tasted it sure came close, a beautiful chewy texture to the oats and topped with brown sugar and stewed rhubarb. And there was that memorable conversation I had with Gideon while driving between Gladstone and Rockhampton. Oh man, we got so excited. Who knew we shared the same passion about water-storage levels in Melbourne dams? And then there was the bonus surprise that in Rockhampton it was Beef Week. The local appliance store featured a window display of vacuum cleaners dressed as cows. The local fish shop had a sign that said, 'Beef Week Special! Fresh Oysters $12. NO BULL!' The shopping plaza had a soundscape of cows mooing, and I've never heard so much animated chat about semen—quantity, quality and availability. And then there was the woman I sat next to on the plane from Mount Isa to Cairns. She was Aboriginal and told me her life story—it was quite amazing. She had lived on an outback station with an abusive white husband but eventually managed to escape, become a nurse, raise her kids and was now on her way to Cairns to speak at an Indigenous health conference. As the plane landed she grabbed my arm and said, 'Can I tell you something? I haven't told anyone this. I *am* speaking at a health conference, but I'm leaving early to go and have a tummy tuck.'

'Wow,' I said to her. And I meant wow.

I wished her well, and we hugged. Sisters united in a secret.

But apart from those highlights things had been pretty low key. We'd spent our days travelling to the next location, did the show at night, sometimes had a drink after—but then again sometimes we didn't. And yet there was no denying I was actually enjoying myself, and, as corny and clichéd as it sounds, goddammit, I felt young again!

But then we got to Townsville and, well, things went a bit weird …

As in I became delusional …

As in I didn't just *feel* young but really and truly believed I *was* young again.

We were staying in a brand-new, swanky, upmarket hotel that overlooked the Townsville marina. Upon our arrival, a young chap at reception wearing a smart brown jacket and a badge declaring his name was Gary leant across the desk, clearly excited out of his mind, and informed me that the Wiggles were also staying there.

My room, on the third storey, was a typical boutique-hotel situation, giving one an impression of space where there was none, the best part being the small balcony where you could sit and watch people and cars being ferried back and forth to Magnetic Island. I marvelled at the 'laundry': hidden out of sight behind dark, polished wood doors, in a nook no bigger than a small cupboard, was a state-of-the-art washing machine that required me to put on my glasses in order to study the complex washing options on a computer-ised screen. Above it was a state-of-the-art clothes dryer. Clothes dryer? Hello? Weren't we in Far North Queensland? A place where the sun shines every day? Which begged the question why have a clothes dryer? Why wouldn't you just hang your underpants over the back of a chair on your balcony?

I found out the answer to that question the next day, when I was forced to go and collect my underpants from Gary, who earlier that morning had kindly retrieved them from the driveway.

That first day I went for a walk and like a moth to a flame was drawn to a beauty salon, where Libbi went to town, rip-ping the hair from my legs, pubic region, upper lip, chin and brows, while a group of monks did some Gregorian chanting in the background. And when it came to a bikini wax Libbi was a perfectionist, because just when I thought it was all over she headed down there with a pair of tweezers.

I said to her, 'Honestly, don't worry about it, Libbi. I'm not that fussed.'

'Denise, I am an artist. You are my canvas. I couldn't bear to send you out into the world knowing I'd left a hair there. What if somebody saw it?'

Libbi, I thought, the only way anyone could possibly see that hair is if I was doing breaststroke in the pool, in the nude, and they were swimming right up my arse behind me. And what's the likelihood of that? I can't do breaststroke.

That night, post-show, we celebrated, because the next day there was no travel and, what's more, it was Mother's Day. We all met in Jeff's room for drinks. We played charades and checked out interesting YouTube videos, one of which involved a woman having sex with a Shetland pony. Each to their own, but I myself didn't think it was entertainment. Someone then decided to roll a joint, but no-one had a match or a lighter and oh my goodness the carry-on until I calmly suggested they use the toaster. We mothers, we just know these things!

It was daylight when, many bottles of wine and packets of crisps later, I headed back to my room. I went straight to sleep. Four hours later I awoke and bounced out of bed, a spring in my step. I walked into the centre of town, where a market was happening. A husband and wife were performing country and western numbers on a small stage.

I rang John. 'Have you got the chook on yet?'

'Yes, Scotty, I've got the chook on. It should be ready by twelve-thirty.'

'And have you rung the home to let them know Mum won't be staying there for lunch?' (Mum was in a locked dementia unit.)

'I haven't rung them yet, but I will.'

'You'd better do it now, John. And you know you have to pick up Mum before midday?'

'Yes, Scotty, don't worry. I'll get her just before twelve.'

'No, John, you have to pick her up before that. Otherwise, the other residents will be sitting down for lunch and Mum won't be able to and she'll get confused.'

'I know that, Scotty. I'll pick her up at five minutes to twelve. It'll be fine.'

'And make sure she wears a coat. You'll have to put it on her. Is Jordie coming?'

'Yes, and we're going to Skype Bonnie.'

Needless to say, Bonnie was alive and well and safely back in Berlin.

'Oh, I wish I could Skype her.'

'Well, if you'd taken your laptop …'

'I know, I know. Maybe she'll ring me for Mother's Day.'

'She can't. She's completely out of credit again.'

'Oh my God, John, you've got to listen to this.' I held the phone up as the country and western duo let rip. The wife was yodelling her head off. 'Could you hear that? Aren't they great?'

'Yes, but Scotty, I'm sorry, I'm going to have to go. I have to catch the shops. I need cream for the apple pie, and I want to get your mum some flowers and chocolates from all of us.'

'Well, give her my love, and I'll try to ring this arvo, but I'm going to some mountain and might be out of range.'

'Okay, love you, Scotty.'

'Love you, John.'

At midday I went to the hotel foyer and sat on the white leather couch. Five minutes later Stu arrived and sat down beside me. 'Scotty.' Stu looked at me. His eyes were sparkling. 'Can I ask you something?'

'Sure.'

'You and John have been together a long time. How do you keep a relationship alive?'

'You work your arse off,' I replied.

Just to give you some indication of how delusional I was becoming, and it does pain me to do so, I managed to interpret the above exchange to mean that Stu was having doubts about his relationship with his stunning, knock-out, utterly drop-dead gorgeous tattooed twenty-four-year-old girlfriend …

Because …

(And here I'm warning you to brace yourselves.)

… he had fallen in love with me.

(Don't say I didn't warn you.)

In my head, this was an entirely possible scenario, because for starters I wasn't me. Well, I *was* me, but I was the me from thirty years ago. In fact, I was an even better, hotter, more funky version of the old me. And Stu and I had been hanging out together a good deal, going on walks, checking out the tourist attractions, often just the two of us, because the rest of the group were usually preoccupied with Facebook business.

Gideon arrived and informed us that no-one else was coming. They were all still in bed recovering from the night before. We headed off in the Tarago. Stu was driving. Gid was in the front passenger seat. I was in the back. It was an uncharacteristically cool and overcast day. We headed out of town, and an hour or so later, when we were halfway up Mount Spec, we decided to stop for a swim at Crystal Creek, a glorious series of deep rock pools featuring a giant waterfall.

I happily threw off my clothes to reveal my G-cup one-piece swimsuit, thrilled in the knowledge that only the day before Libbi had denuded me of unsightly body hair. As for my sun-damaged skin and all my goobies and age-related warts, they didn't bother me, not in the least, because as far as I was concerned I didn't have any, because I was a young, slim, fit and vibrant woman with flawless skin who glowed with joie de vivre and hope for the future.

Gideon stood on the rocks taking photos while Stu and I dived into the icy-cold water. I unashamedly showed off, gaily freestyling, backstroking and butterflying. At one point I dived beneath the surface and suddenly shot my legs up out of the water, where I enthusiastically began opening and closing them like a pair of scissors, à la Esther Williams.

Stu and I then disappeared behind the waterfall, where we floated together in the dark cave, hidden from sight by the thunderous curtain of cascading water. It was freezing cold. We shivered and laughed. Laughed and shivered. Shivered and laughed. It was obvious to me that there was a strong sexual tension between us. Why wouldn't there be? We were both young, we were both hot, we were both away from our loved ones, and we were both frolicking in a dark, thunderous water-fall situation.

Later that afternoon, at the top of the mountain, we went to a cafe and drank tea and ate scones with jam and cream. I was wearing Stu's checked woollen jacket that he had lent me. It was too small, but who cared? Not me.

At one point Stu gazed intently into my eyes and said, 'Oh Scotty, I wish you were my lover.'

(Now, the fact that what Stu actually said was 'Oh Scotty, I wish you were my mother,' the point being it was Mother's Day, and yet I clearly heard the word 'lover', indicates just how delusional I had become.)

It was when we began our descent of the mountain and I saw a sign informing me there was 18 kilometres of winding road ahead that I began to feel quite ill and to wish I hadn't drunk quite so much the night before, yet alone just scoffed a scone the size of a small cauliflower. And it wasn't just a winding road; it was a corkscrew situation—steep and narrow and tight.

And so began our long descent. We went around and around and around and around and around and around and around and around and around and around and around and around and around and around and around and around until …

Oh no, oh, Jesus Christ, fuck me dead—excuse the language, but at the time that was my exact thought—I saw another sign.

Sixteen kilometres of winding road to go.

And so around we went again and again and again and again and again and again and again and again and again and again and again and again and again and again and again and again until finally the road was straight.

And that's when I said, 'Do you think you could pull over, Stu?'

I got out of the van and there, by the side of the road, with the magnificent sugarcane fields of Far North Queensland as a backdrop, I collapsed onto all fours and vomited my guts up. I vomited until there was nothing more to vomit, except that I did vomit again, and then again, until there was just a thread of bile swinging from my mouth.

And because of my age and the intensity of the vomits, I also wet my pants. And, to my great amazement, I also started menstruating, which was nothing short of a miracle, as I hadn't done that for at least a year and a half.

Slowly I stood up; my whole body was shaking, my head was thumping, and my arthritic ankle had gone, forcing me to drag my leg behind me like Quasimodo. I slumped against the front passenger door of the van. Gideon and Stu were looking straight ahead—a tactful gesture on their part.

I banged my fists on the window. 'I'm not twenty-four, am I?'

Neither Stu nor Gideon answered this question, which was entirely appropriate given there was no happy answer to be had.

'I'm not twenty-four. I'm fifty-four. I'm fifty-fucking-four.'

Gently, I slid open the back door and got into the van, and as night fell we drove back towards Townsville in silence, until finally Stu looked at me via the rear-vision mirror and said, 'By the way, Scotty, happy Mother's Day.'

Then one of the boys snorted like a pig, and it broke the ice and we all laughed until we had tears streaming down our faces.

And that was it: my awakening. It was like a spiritual slap across the face, the sort of slap that wakes you up and makes you come back to life, rise to the surface and gulp for air. And, as I sat in the back of that van, covered in vomit, blood and urine, I felt joy—pure, unadulterated joy.

Time had got away from us. We had to hightail it back to the hotel, quickly change and race to meet the others at the theatre. I was as white as a sheet and still shaking. I performed my set and came offstage to discover that Stu had found an old mattress backstage and had dragged it into my dressing room. I turned off the light and lay down until it was time for the curtain call, at the end of the show. As I lay there in the dark on that putrid mattress I could barely suppress the happiness I felt. It was … well, it was a state of euphoria. I couldn't recall having ever experienced anything quite like it. It was as though a tremendous burden had finally been lifted from my shoulders and for the first time in my life I felt free. I had no idea what burden I had been freed from. All I knew was that something truly significant had taken place.

Back in my hotel room I rang John. The chook had been a triumph. The apple pie had been fantastic. Mum had had a great time.

'And how was your day, Scotty?'

'It was good. Really good.'

chapter one

Beginnings

I grew up in an outer Melbourne suburb called Greensborough, so named because it was green. And that's about all you need to know. Put it this way: Greensborough in the late 1950s was hardly known for its wow factor. And that suited my mother down to the ground, because Margaret Scott loved the ordinary.

In fact, I'd go so far as to say that if there were a Goddess of Ordinariness my mother would have lain prostrate and worshipped at her feet, were it not for the fact that it would have drawn unwanted attention. She was a quiet, devoted, no-nonsense, no-fuss sort of woman whose favourite sayings were 'Neat as a pin,' 'Not a hair out of place' and 'She was a real little lady.' She was also often heard to say, 'When in Rome …' She never finished the sentence; she didn't have to. All she had to do was purse her lips and raise her eyebrows ever so slightly and you just knew Rome was our war service home and the Romans were in fact one woman and her name was Marg Scott.

Mum set the rules, and my sister and I obeyed them. We never disobeyed her. We never argued with her. Ever. And the only time my father and mother argued was of a Saturday evening when Dad would roll home from Dawson's Hotel having drunk too much in a futile attempt to ease the pain of his beloved Heidelberg West football team being thrashed yet again. My mother didn't like to argue. She didn't like the boat to be rocked. She liked things to be calm and ordered and uneventful.

My mother's house was a spick-and-span humble home with no clutter, and there was never anything out of place. One of her favourite stories was about the time a neighbour had called in. 'It wasn't even half past eight in the morning, and would you believe, as luck would have it, I was dressed, the dishes were done, the beds were made. I'd even polished the kitchen floors. I felt tremendous.'

Every evening at 7 pm my sister, Julie, and I set the table, and every evening we ate a tasty home-cooked meal such as stew and mash followed by custard and tinned fruit. There was never any need for Jenny Craig in our house, because portions were always moderate—not because my mother was ungenerous but because she did not believe in excess. Thanks to the fact that pubs closed at 6 pm (oh, what a sad and dreary life it must have been) my father was usually home for 'tea', unless of course he had footy training or a footy meeting or footy crisis talks to attend at the Heidelberg West footy ground. There was always a clean and ironed tablecloth, and we always sat in the same place, my father and sister on one side, my mother and I on the other. No fuss. No bother. No surprises.

Dinner conversation was subtle, as in very subtle, as in we didn't say much. And we were all comfortable with that. I guess we had to be: there was no alternative. Politics was never mentioned. Nor were world events. And as for religion, forget it. Sport? Dad would have loved a discussion, but the rest of us weren't in the least interested. Hopes, dreams, ambitions? Get over yourself. And we never asked questions. I believe it was my mother who taught us this art, stemming from her firm belief in the saying 'What you don't know won't hurt you.'

Thus, in our house, conversations were more like strings of statements, often completely unrelated. For instance, as we sat at the kitchen table eating our tea, my mother might say something along the lines of 'Mr Sawyer died today.'

And then a minute or so later my father would say, 'Beautiful dinner, Marg.'

And then after another pause my sister would say, 'A girl in my class fainted this morning.'

And then Mum would say, 'Trust him to die on my shift.'

And Dad would say, 'What's for dessert, Marg?', which admittedly was a question but they really were rare.

And I would say, 'Gee, I wish I could get a horse.'

And my mother would say, 'Tinned fruit and custard.'

You get the drift.

Every two weeks my mother had her hair set and every six months had her hair permed at Anne Barnes Beauty Salon. In between appointments she would maintain her 'do' by wearing hair curlers and hairnet to bed.

I had no problem with my mother having a Queen Elizabeth–inspired perm, but I did have a problem when she decided I should have one as well. She performed the deed herself, having purchased a Toni Home Perm kit from the local chemist that she enthusiastically applied to my thick, straight blonde hair.

To this day I recall the moment when I first saw my reflection in the mirror. You never really do get over a shock like that. There I was, a seven-year-old girl with the hairdo of an eighty-year-old woman. I wanted to cry out in horror but dared not for fear of upsetting my mother. I sensed she was equally horrified but couldn't show it, because after all there was nothing to be done. 'So snap out of it, Denise, and come out from behind that bush and get to school immediately.'

My mother was not without passion. She loved gardening and she loved sewing. She made my sister and me all our clothes; hence, we wore identical outfits, which was cute though a little embarrassing come adolescence. When I went to hospital to have my tonsils out she made me and my doll matching nighties.

Without doubt her greatest triumphs on the sewing front were the suits she made for Julie and me when we were eleven and nine years old respectively. Mine was blue. My sister's was pink. They were waisted dresses with matching jackets that were covered in lace.

My mother had first seen them in the newspaper. They were featured in an advertisement for Georges, an upmarket department store in the city. She was so taken with them that she determined to replicate them for her girls. She became quite feverish and obsessed about it, her machine whirring at all hours of the day and night, and when she wasn't sewing she was on the phone, organising to have the skirts sent away to be perma-pleated, or tracking down the tools needed to make the hand-covered buttons and belts.

The finished outfits were quite literally a breathtaking success. Our next-door neighbour Beryl Higgins, upon seeing them, gasped and clutched the front of her cardigan as though about to have a heart attack as my mother, not normally one to blow her own trumpet, proudly declared, 'They look just like the ones in Georges. And do you know how much those ones cost?'

'How much, Marg?'

'Twenty-two guineas!'

'Twenty-two guineas!'

'And do you know how much I made the girls' suits for?'

'How much, Marg?'

'Two pound ten.'

They really were beautiful. It was such a shame we never went anywhere we could wear them.

And Mum loved smoking. She was a packet-a-day gal, Albany cigarettes were her choice of smoking pleasure. Every morning when she wasn't doing night shift, Dad would deliver her a cup of tea and a cigarette in bed.

Mum was particularly passionate about swearing. Passionately opposed to it, that is. She loathed it, although on occasion she was heard to say 'Bugger,' when chopping wood and a splinter flew into her forehead, for instance. (Having grown up in the country, my mother was a mighty axe wielder, and it was her job to fuel our open fire. Dad, being a city slicker, was banned from the wood heap.)

One day when my sister and I were walking home from primary school we were stopped by the high-school bullies—a group of adolescent girls—who had spread themselves out in a line across the street, daring us to pass them.

My sister and I froze in our tracks.

The leader of the gang walked over to me. She looked down at me and hissed, 'Do you know what "fuck" means?'

I shook my head. Of course I didn't know what it meant. I'd only been on the planet six years and didn't get out much. I'd never heard of the word, yet alone heard anyone say it, which in hindsight was nothing short of a miracle, given that my father was a lifetime member of the Heidelberg West Football Club.

'You go home and ask your mother what "fuck" means.'

I nodded agreement.

'You'd better do it; otherwise, you'll be sorry. Well, go on, what are you waiting for?'

My sister and I walked in the back door.

Mum was vacuuming the enclosed veranda, which she had recently had covered in a brown synthetic carpet. She had her back to us. The upright hoover was extremely noisy and I had to yell. 'MUM, DO YOU KNOW WHAT "FUCK" MEANS?'

The vacuum cleaner whirred to a meaningful sort of silence.

Slowly, my mother turned around. I could not believe my eyes. Surely her perm wasn't literally standing on end? But that was how it seemed, such was the look of horror on my mother's face. And then she spoke with a voice I'd never heard before—cold, chilling and deadly serious. 'You must never, ever, *ever* say that word again. Do you hear me? It is a terrible, *terrible* word, and if a policeman ever hears you say it you'll be put in jail.'

In my mother's eyes, swear words were nothing short of criminal, especially when spoken by a lady.

My mother's determination to avoid anything that upset the calm progression of daily life knew no bounds, her reaction to the news of a murder being a superb example of a woman resolved to keep a lid on the excitement of life. It wasn't just any murder; it was Greensborough's very own Desperate Housewives situation. I only knew about it because of my uncanny ability in, and absolute devotion to, the ancient art of eavesdropping. As a child I did it all the time.

One day a few women from the St Mary's Mothers Club, all with identical perms—except for Mrs Alcock, who bucked the system with a teased French roll—rocked up to our house, each armed with a portable sewing machine. Their mission? To make young boys trousers to sell at the St Mary's school fete. Mrs Alcock handed out pieces of fabric already cut into various shapes and gave instructions on how to assemble them. With heads bent low, right foot delicately placed just above the treadle and steady hands poised ready to guide the grey fabric under the needle, they waited for Mrs Alcock to give the word, and then away they went. I was in the lounge room at the time pretending to read, but in reality I was fully focussed on the ladies, fascinated by them. I kept sneaking a look through the servery, a hole

Mum had had cut in the wall so that when she was in the kitchen, which she nearly always was, she could still see the TV in the lounge.

Eventually, all the machines came to a halt, and I heard one of the mothers, Mrs Schultze, comment, 'Oh no. Will you look at that? My inside pocket—it's facing the wrong way. Oh well, I guess that'll come in handy for some little boy with a back-to-front hand.'

All the mothers roared.

And then another mother said, 'What about Valerie Thompson killing her husband?'

Hello! What? Mrs Thompson killed her husband? My eyes widened to the size of cricket balls. Mrs Thompson was one of the sweetest mothers at the school. And one of the most religious. She was always putting flowers on the altar …

'Apparently, he was passed out on the couch, as usual, and she just bashed him to death with a softball bat.'

My eyes were now the size of basketballs. I pictured teeny tiny Mrs Thompson swinging a softball bat, smashing her husband's skull to pieces.

'He deserved it, though. He was a brute to her.'

'Anyone like a cuppa?'

That was what my mother said upon hearing the news of Mr Thompson's demise.

Even the near death of her daughter couldn't extract any public emotional response from my mother. I was four years old at the time and having a bath with my sister while Mum was in the kitchen preparing dinner.

Suddenly, my sister started screaming.

My mother raced into the bathroom to find Julie standing in the bath staring down at me in horror. My lifeless body lay submerged under the water, my eyes, as Mum later recalled, 'wide open, big as saucers, unblinking, just staring up at the ceiling.'

Mum heaved me out of the bath, shook the bejesus out of me and ferociously slapped life back into my face.

Half an hour later, as we sat at the table eating tea, all my mother said to my father was, 'Well, Russ, one thing's for sure: that's the last time I give Denise a sleeping tablet *before* she has her bath.'

Paradoxically for a woman who strove to be ordinary, my mother contradicted the 1950s housewife stereotype by having a job. She was a nurses aide at the Deloraine Aged Care hospital, conveniently located across the road from our house. She hadn't wanted to do it. Goodness gracious me, no. She wanted to be a stay-at-home mum, but that pesky Matron Barnes (mother to Anne, she of Anne Barnes Beauty Salon fame) hounded my mother, sermonising about the elderly people needing her care and attention. She didn't bother to mention it would also be handy to have a nurse living across the road; any time someone couldn't make it to work, all Matron would have to do was pop her head out the window and yell 'MARG!' My mother finally succumbed and started working at the hospital, and she loved it.

When we were toddlers she did night shift, arriving home at 7 am just in time to farewell my father as he headed off to work. My mother would then get into bed and sleep for a few hours. Child care wasn't a problem: Mum would simply put my sister and me on the bed with her, with a few books and toys for our amusement, and there we'd stay until she woke up.

When we started school my mother swapped to the morning shift, 7 am to 12.30 pm, five days a week. This meant that from the age of five I'd get myself up, make my own breakfast (usually a sweet biscuit and cup of tea) and walk myself to school; my sister, sick of waiting for me, always headed off earlier. I didn't like school—it interfered with my fantasy world—and often I would feign sickness so I could stay at home and play. Julie would have to go across the road and deliver the news to Mum, and, since she was more often than not in the middle of bathing a patient at the time, there was nothing she could do about it.

I loved having the house to myself! As soon as I heard Julie shut the front door I'd jump out of bed and put on my ballet slippers. (I only ever went to two lessons before giving up in disgust. I didn't like the teacher telling me what to do; I much preferred a free-form, interpretative approach to dance.) I'd turn on the radio in the kitchen and, still in my pyjamas, immerse myself in the classical music and dance for a good couple of hours. I'd then swap my ballet slippers for bedroom slippers, arrange my face in a suitably sad-sack expression and head across to the hospital, where I'd sit in the staffroom with my mother and the rest of the nursing staff while they drank tea, ate Savoy biscuits and cheese, and chain-smoked cigarettes.

Even better than having the house to myself was when my mother had a day off work and made us porridge. And even better than that was the thought of staying at home and having Mum all to myself. But it was usually only a thought, because my mother wasn't so keen on the idea. No matter how well I acted, she refused to believe I was ill and would force me out of the house. Force! There I was, a small girl with large blue eyes, beside myself, sobbing with the tragedy of it all. Mum had to march behind me, not exactly hitting me on the bottom, rather tapping it, forcing me ever onwards until we got to the school gate, at which point she would be mortified to discover that she was still in her dressing gown.

My mother was a big fan of routine, and every weekday come 2.30 pm she would have her afternoon nap for an hour. If ever I was lucky enough to be home at that time I would get into bed with her. I loved it, although in hindsight it probably annoyed the hell out of Mum, who was no doubt desperate for a bit of time to herself. So great was my love of sharing an arvo nap with her that once, when I was fifteen and loved my waist-length hair more than life itself, and my mother had announced there'd been an outbreak of nits at her work while furiously scratching her scalp, I still had a nap with her—although I did insist on wearing a shower cap.

My mother's arvo nap was sacred. Nothing and no-one messed with it, not even a raging bushfire.

I was nine years old and sitting in class at St Mary's one day when our teacher announced we were to go home immediately; the school was being evacuated. I walked home alone, as by then Julie had started secondary school and was in the city.

Walking across the top of the cutting that cleaved Grimshaw Street in two, I saw flames in the distance. The sky was orange. My little legs, already red raw with eczema behind the knees and between my thighs—a ghastly and possibly unnecessary image, but hey, it's the truth, and I feel it adds a certain pathos to the scene—prickled with heat and stress and fear.

I hurried down our driveway and once inside the back door headed straight for my mother's bedroom. I knew she would be there having her afternoon nap. Sure enough, there she was, lying on the bed, her Queen Elizabeth perm rising and falling in a steady, calm rhythm on the pillow.

'Mum …'

She sat up immediately and looked at me in dazed shock. 'What are you doing here?'

'We were sent home. There's terrible fires and they say we should get out.'

My mother sighed. Deeply. 'Oh, wouldn't you know it. I've just spent over an hour and a half washing the front porch, and now the whole house is going to burn down. What a waste of time that was.'

And then Mum put her head back on the pillow.

I had been kind of hoping she might do something. I don't know what exactly—maybe get us both out of there before we *burnt to death*?

The phone rang.

I ran to answer it.

It was my father. He'd heard about the fires and wanted to get home to us, but all the roads had been closed off; no-one was allowed in.

There was a knock at the front door. Oh, thank God. A rescuer, perhaps?

I ran to open it.

It was Matron Barnes. She looked mad with panic, her stiff, starched nursing veil sitting skew-whiff on top of her head. She raced into the house, yelling, 'Where's your mother?'

Immediately, my mother came flying out of the bedroom—a nurse heeding the call to arms.

'Hurry, Marg. We have to evacuate the patients.'

And at that my mother raced back to the bedroom, put on her sandals and took off across the road.

I stood there in shock. Was my mother for real? Was she really going to save geriatrics and let *me* be incinerated?

A minute later she came flying back into the house.

What a relief. She had come to her senses after all and was going to get me out of there.

Mum ran straight past me, into her bedroom. I followed and found her putting a skirt on over the top of her shorts. 'I don't want the patients to see my varicose veins.'

And with that once more she was gone.

There is an old adage that says such things are sent to try us, and blow me down if a bit of the old Henry Lawson 'Drover's wife' pioneering spirit didn't kick in and give me the courage to take action. I got my mother's round cane shopping basket, which was decorated with a yellow plastic flower, and began packing. A Hawaiian shirt, pair of underpants, shorts and socks for Dad; a rose-patterned frock, stilettos, bra, pants, suspender belt and stockings for Mum; for my sister and me a pair of underpants, shorts, top and, even though we were too old for them, our Cindy dolls.

I then rounded up our grey Persian cat, Fluffy, and our out-of-control labrador, Prince, and went and sat on the newly washed front porch and waited. For what? I wasn't sure. I guess I hoped that someone might take pity on a little girl with a basket, a dog and a cat, not to mention eczema, and maybe even offer her a lift to safety.

But no-one went past.

I hung on to my dog and cat by the fur on their necks with all my might, but my hands became drenched with sweat and the animals became restless and slipped away from me. But I stayed seated on the porch and watched Mum load patients into the back of ambulances. Suddenly I heard fire trucks, their bells madly ringing: they were close.

And so were the flames. I could see them clearly now. They seemed to be travelling fast.

And that was when Matron Barnes came racing out of the hospital, this time with her veil sticking straight up in the air. She was screaming, 'The fires! They're here! They're at the bottom of our street!'

I ran across the road to my mother, and we all stood in the hallway of the hospital. I couldn't believe we were going to die and those old people were going to live. A minute or so later a fireman appeared before us, his big gold hat a shiny, masculine symbol of hope. He assured us the fires were under control.

Eventually, all the patients were returned to their beds, Fluffy and Prince re-emerged unscathed, and I raced home and quickly put away the clothes I had packed. I didn't want my mother to know I had taken such action; she might think it silly. Nor did I want her to know that, at that moment, in the hallway of the hospital, when I was sure we were going to be burnt to death, I had felt so frightened I wanted to scream my lungs out. Of course, I hadn't, because Mum wouldn't have approved of such hysteria. I also didn't want her to know that, when I'd been sitting on the front porch watching her lift old people into the ambulance, under my breath I'd been whimpering, 'What about me, Mum?'

As well as insomnia and eczema, as a child I also suffered severe asthma attacks. Mum was usually pretty cool about it. She would calmly sit there rubbing my back, saying stuff like 'Just wait until I've finished my cigarette, Denise, and I'll plug in your Ventolin machine.'

In the lead-up to the Christmas of 1965 my asthma was so severe that my mother *nearly* called an ambulance; but of course she didn't, because calling an ambulance meant making a fuss, and, what with her daughter wheezing to death, life was already stressful enough without having an attention-seeking ambulance, siren blaring, screaming up the street, bringing all the neighbours out to see what was going on.

During that period my mother or father stayed with me in my bedroom all night, every night, keeping an eye on me, making sure I was breathing okay (although Dad always fell asleep and snored his head off, but hey, his heart was in the right place). By Christmas they were both exhausted, so instead of having the usual extended-family lunch in our aluminium garage on Christmas Day it was decided we would go to a restaurant.

When the plans were made my parents had assumed I'd be able to come, but I was too sick, so my mother, always one for a practical solution, went across the road to the hospital and came back with the news that, 'as luck would have it, Mrs Cooper died last night.'

And so there I was, nine years old, sitting up in Mrs Cooper's recently vacated bed in the aged-care hospital, trying my best to sing Christmas carols with all the old ladies, but I just couldn't. My wheezing little chest was unable to muster the strength.

Given that my father tended towards unpredictable, exhibitionist, some might say insane behaviour, it would be easy to assume he was a major obstacle to my mother leading an ordinary life. But in fact it was quite the opposite—my dad's behaviour gave Mum the opportunity to be as ordinary as she ever hoped to be.

Marg and Russ first met and consequently fell in love at a dance at Heidelberg Town Hall during the Second World War. Mum was in the army, working as a nurses aide at the Heidelberg Repat Hospital. Dad was in the navy. They both loved music, especially big band ballroom numbers, and my father liked to dance as much as Mum did—the Pride of Erin, a flowing waltz, a smooth foxtrot—according to all reports they sizzled on the dance floor. However, after a few beers my father was inclined to suddenly, without warning, break into a full-on free-form jitterbugging frenzy. This involved a lot of twirling and throwing himself on the floor, not to mention throwing Mum over his shoulder and under his legs and to either side of his hips, his large eyes popping out of his head with the excitement. At this point my mother would always, with an air of resolute acceptance—after all, what could she do?—go and sit down, leaving Dad to carry on solo. This pattern continued for their entire marriage and always resulted in Dad lying on the lounge room floor the following day, unable to move, because 'a man's done his bloody back in.' My mother would roll her eyes, step over the top of him and get on with her domestic tasks.

They were a Yin and Yang love story if ever there was one—Mum provided Dad with a calm and stable home, while he brought the crazy and unconventional to her life. This left my mother free to be as restrained, understated and low key as she desired, safe in the knowledge that her husband would take care of all the exciting stuff in their lives.

However, something that did make it tricky for my mum to live under the radar was our family car, or, rather, van. It didn't actually belong to my father; it was his work vehicle. His job was delivering smallgoods, transporting frankfurters and strass (large rolls of Strasbourg sausage) to shops all over Melbourne. He worked for Star Smallgoods and drove a combi van covered in animated sausages that wore boater hats and tap shoes and had cartoon bubbles saying, 'Eat us up we're yummy, yummy for your tummy.'

Since we didn't have our own car, we went everywhere in Dad's work van. It was legendary. Dad was famous for being able to single-handedly pick up and deliver the entire Watsonia Girls Calisthenics team in the back of that van, and often drove us to and from our various concerts and competitions.

There would be ten of us, all dressed in leotards, marching-girl tan thickly painted on our legs, rolling around in the back of the van with the rear door half-open, trying to hang on to one another for support as Dad merrily sailed around corners. Occasionally he'd brake suddenly, causing the rear door to slam shut, leaving us in pitch-black darkness with no oxygen supply, all of us screaming to no avail, as my father couldn't hear us. When my sister was enrolled in Catholic Ladies' College in East Melbourne, where parents tended to be doctors and lawyers, come school speech night, while everyone else rolled up in their Mercedes or Jaguar, the Scott family arrived in the sausage van. But most memorable of all the sausage van excursions was when we went to the circus in the neighbouring suburb of Watsonia.

Given that it was a combi and there were four of us to share the front seat, seating arrangements were very precise. Naturally, my father sat behind the wheel. Next to him was my sister, one leg on either side of the four-on-the-floor gearstick. Next to her was my mother, who sat with her left leg crossed over her right, her left buttock lifted slightly off the seat. I sat next to my mother, as far forward on the seat as was possible without falling off, my hands gripping the handle on the dashboard and my nose pressed up against the windscreen. Oh, the good old days before seatbelts were invented. Such fun times.

On the night of the circus, like everyone, we parked in a paddock nearby. It was a stormy night and during the show it poured with rain. Returning to the paddock afterwards we were confronted with a sea of sunken vehicles, every one of them bogged knee-deep in mud. After a few attempts involving wheels spinning and mud flying and fathers cursing and children crying and mothers being sensible, everyone gave up and walked home.

Except for us. 'A man can't leave the van here. I've got black puddings to deliver first thing in the morning.'

And so, like a modern-day superhero, my father told his women to wait in the van while he went back to the circus to get a shovel.

It was dark and wet and lonely as we sat in that paddock in total silence, until my mother muttered, 'Oh my godfathers.' I followed her gaze and saw my father marching towards us. He didn't have a shovel.

He had an elephant.

A circus hand instructed the elephant to wrap its trunk around the front bumper bar. Given our seating arrangements and the fact that combi vans have no front engine, this meant I was now quite literally eyeball to eyeball with the elephant. Slowly it heaved us up and up and up, sucking the van out of the mud until we were high in the air. And then, moving backwards, it dragged us across the paddock and gently deposited us onto dry land.

My father duly thanked the elephant and its trainer, and we drove home in silence apart from when my father said, 'Good night, hey, Mother?'

My mother rolled her eyes and said, 'Not bad.'

My mother not only took vicarious pleasure in my father's extrovert behaviour; she sometimes encouraged it outright:

after all, it was Marg who made Russ his very own clown suit. She created it in secret and gave it to him for Christmas one year. Even more remarkable was that my father used to wear it—often. (And yes, the fact that John was a clown when I first met him, albeit a professional one, has not escaped me.)

Dad's clown suit, designed and lovingly stitched by Mum, was your classic multicoloured, patchwork number with large pom-pom buttons, a ruffled collar and a cone-shaped hat that stayed on his head courtesy of elastic under the chin. He had clown make-up that he applied in a rather, shall we say, free and easy, intuitive manner, never having attended a make-up class in his life.

The clown suit was made more noteworthy by the fact that my father wasn't a clown. What I mean is, my father had no clowning skills whatsoever: he couldn't juggle or play an instrument or do anything that in any way resembled a clowning activity. All he had going for him was a general joie de vivre and a complete lack of inhibition, especially after a few drinks. My mother enjoyed my father being a clown—mostly. She sometimes even laughed, and from her small but evident smile it was obvious she appreciated all the happiness my father's poorly performed but well-intentioned, usually alcohol-influenced, clown antics brought to any event.

Dad's behaviour was considered, if not exactly normal, completely predictable in my extended family, and in fact it wasn't until Dad appeared in his clown suit at my sixteenth birthday party and Glenn D, leader of the Burra Boys, who joy of joys had chosen my party to gatecrash, said to me, 'Who the fuck is that mental case?' that it occurred to me that perhaps my father's behaviour was a little odd.

My mother didn't enjoy my father being a clown at RSL picnics; nor did his daughters. All of us, in the end, refused to go. We couldn't take it any more—it was way too distressing to see such a beautiful, well-meaning man being pummelled and kicked and dragged to the ground, his clown suit torn to shreds, by feral kids whose parents were too pissed to notice or care that their darling child was killing Mr Clown.

Sometimes my mother and father worked as a double act; it was a seamless performance. It required my father to pretend to be a doctor. When Mum was doing night shift at the hospital on her own, a common event in those days, and a patient fell out of bed or became distressed and needed restraining, she always called on Dad to help. Without hesitation, he would dramatically throw on his white smallgoods jacket, conveniently covered in blood stains, and race across the road, whereupon Mum would exclaim, 'Good of you to get here so quickly, Dr Scott.'

'Always a pleasure, Nurse.'

Together, they would carefully get the patient back into bed, my dad offering comforting words of reassurance, more often than not getting the patient to smile and comment, 'What a lovely doctor.'

'Yes, isn't he?' Mum would agree.

Things weren't quite so harmonious when it came to religion. In case it's not already obvious, my mother was an extremely conservative woman and accordingly insisted my sister and I be brought up as strict Catholics. Nothing unusual about that, except that neither of our parents were Catholic. Dad had no religion, and Mum always referred to herself as a Catholic but never went to church.

Actually, I exaggerate. When my sister and I made our first communion and confirmation, Mum was in attendance.

My mother was brought up in a strict Catholic family in a small country town, and while it was one thing for her to reach adulthood and turn her back on religion, when it came to her daughters they had to be Catholic, no two ways about it. I guess she was covering her bases, worried that if we died and went to hell it would be her fault for not raising us Catholic, and that responsibility was too much for any mother to bear.

Uncharacteristically, my father argued with my mother about this. He had no choice. There was a principle at stake, although it had nothing to do with religion. Then again, come to think of it, it had everything to do with religion: it was all about Australian Rules football.

As fortune, or rather misfortune, would have it, on the very same day my mother enrolled my sister at St Mary's Catholic School, my father arrived home and announced he had been elected secretary of the Heidelberg West Football Club. What has to be understood is that for my father this was akin to becoming prime minister of Australia. He could not have been more honoured or proud or emotional. It was a life-time dream come true.

'Over my dead body.' That was all my mother had to say about the matter.

'Well, Marg, if I can't be secretary of the Heidelberg West Football Club then the girls can't be Catholic.' That was how much being secretary of the footy club meant to my dad—he dared to defy my mother (a rare and memorable event if ever there was one)—and without further ado he marched my sister down to the state school and enrolled her there.

This was war.

Marg versus Russ.

Wife versus husband.

Catholic dogs versus state-school frogs.

Long story short, we kids became Catholic *and* Dad became secretary of the Heidelberg West Football Club, going on to hold every position available, including the presidency. From then on, my father often stood in the lounge room and addressed his beloved boys from the footy club, who were famous for being thrashed by a phenomenal number of points, week after week. The fact that there were never any footballers in our lounge room in no way diminished my father's moving and passionate oration, at times pleading, at times motivating, at times even crying, but always building to the same passionate climax: 'All a man asks is that you do your bloody best, and a man wouldn't be surprised if you take home the flag this year.'

Sometimes Mum would be sitting at the kitchen table having a cup of tea with a neighbour when Dad delivered one of these speeches.

'Who is Russ talking to, Marg?'

'No-one,' was all she ever said.

My dad's extended family wasn't exactly ordinary, either. And yet Mum loved them almost as much as she loved Dad. She often used to talk about how lucky she was to be part of such a great family. She adored his father, my Grandpa Scott, and despite being so famously undemonstrative she would some-times sit on Grandpa's knee and cuddle him. My dad was the eldest of nine—five boys, four girls. They grew up in a small working-class home in Heidelberg West, and extended-family gatherings were regular events. My mother often took charge of organising these, including the big doozy on Christmas Day, which was regularly held in our aluminium garage, with trestle tables and extra chairs borrowed from the footy club.

On such occasions Aunty Dot, who'd had breast cancer and subsequently a mastectomy, often popped her false breast on top of her head, the best part being that she never referred to it.

Uncle Doug wore milk-bottle-bottomed glasses that mag-nified his already large eyes to the size of Mr Magoo's. Every time I said hello to him he'd peer at me through his thick glasses and say, 'Do I know you?'

Uncle Len's specialty was to announce, 'I was at the doc-tor's last week ...' and then away he would go, hooking us into his story. Twenty minutes later, as the story reached its climax, we would groan with the realisation that this was not a per-sonal story at all but just a reworking of a classic joke with a suitably anticlimactic cornball punchline.

Uncle Frank was a milkman who on the side sold Avon products and enjoyed knitting, cable-stitch jumpers being his specialty. Unlike his brothers, who could drink and drink and get funnier and funnier, Uncle Frank only had to have one glass before bursting into tears—of happiness or sadness. Either way his jowls wobbled with the emotion.

At some point, usually after a liberal amount of beer had been consumed, the five brothers—Russ, Doug, Frank, Len and Ken—would perform a medley of tunes, always beginning with 'Popeye the sailor man'. As accompaniment, Uncle Doug would lift his foot dramatically onto a chair and proceed to roll up his trouser leg, revealing a skinny, pale-white calf muscle. He'd then blow on his fingers, rub his hands together, shake them out, and, with a good deal of flourishing, commence to play his calf muscle like a double bass. Doug would also play our Persian cat, Fluffy, by holding her backwards under his armpit and blowing into the end of her tail.

Uncle Ken, the youngest brother, always brought the house down with his rendition of a Canadian song called 'Mule train'. He used to accompany himself by bashing himself over the head with a scone tray to create the sound of a whip cracking. By the time he reached the final chorus he would be marching up and down on the spot, singing his heart out, continually hitting himself with the tray until blood streamed down his face.

These Scott-family gatherings were where I saw Mum at her happiest, obviously revelling in belonging to such a fun-filled family. The boisterous clan allowed her to keep her head down and remain focussed on baking and serving her home-made sausage rolls, enjoying the antics without having to get too involved herself.

My mother's family was a different story. There was always mystery surrounding them—I could never quite figure out how they all fitted together. As a child what I did know was that my mother was the youngest of four children. Her siblings, Bill, Ted and May, were much older than her; in fact, as a child my mother had lived with May and her husband, Jim, and their four children until she left at eighteen to go to the big smoke and join the army. I'd always assumed the reason my mother lived with her big sister was because she (and consequently May and her two older brothers) were orphans. But I'd never really bothered to wonder about my mother's living arrangements; that was just how they were.

May's eldest daughter, Noreen, was only two years younger than my mother, and they were extremely close—they virtually grew up together. Until my mother left home, she shared a double bed with Noreen in the sleep-out in the backyard. They did their chores together, rode their pushbikes everywhere together, and as adolescents loved to go to the local cinema together. When Noreen married she moved nearby to Shepparton with her truck-driving husband, who was also a ballroom dancing champion. They had two sons, whom we saw a good deal of in the early days. I loved Noreen (still do!). I used to take great delight in calling her Cousin Nor, because of course she was my cousin, but old enough to be my aunt.

Apart from Noreen, we didn't see Mum's family very often—certainly nowhere near as much as we saw the Scotts. Once, sometimes twice, a year we'd climb aboard the sausage van and tootle up the Hume, heading northwards to Tatura, 180 kilometres from Melbourne, to visit May and Jim. The journey took days—at least, that was what it felt like. It was always at least 35 degrees Celsius when we travelled, the four of us sitting so close that the sweat made us stick together. We'd all hold our breath and silently pray, willing the van onwards as it wheezed and spluttered its way up Pretty Sally Hill. Sometimes, as we neared the top, she (the van was always 'she') would start to roll backwards, a rather terrifying moment, especially for the poor car travelling behind us.

I was often carsick, and once it was so hot I became totally dehydrated, to the point where Mum declared, 'Russ, we need to get to a hospital.' Of course, there wasn't a hospital, so instead we went to a pub, where I was carried out the back to an old lean-to bathroom. Mum filled the large claw-foot bath with water and I lay in it, cooling off. My sister came to see me with a packet of crisps. She gave me one, and it stuck to the roof of my mouth because I had no saliva.

I loved staying at May's house. May was quiet—extremely so. She never wore make-up, always wore a full apron with bib, was a ferociously neat housekeeper and was kind, loving and gentle. She spent her days and nights doing chores. Her home was humble, verging on the austere. There were few knick-knacks, the odd crucifix on the wall, an oval, framed picture of Jesus baring his sacred heart and a large photo in an ornate dark-wood frame of a greyhound wearing a blue sash. The dog had belonged to May and her husband and at some point had won a major race. It was a high point of their lives and was often reminisced about.

There was a wood-fire cooker that was constantly burning, summer and winter. May would bake delicious, wholesome country foods, and there was always a pot of soup on the go. Above the cooker, in pride of place on the mantelpiece, was a beautiful old clock that gonged on the hour and *tick-tocked* loudly as we ate our tea in silence (because Jim didn't approve of talking at the table).

As much as I loved staying with May, the *tick-tocking* of that clock on the mantelpiece gave me a feeling that in this house time stood still. These were people who led ordinary lives, without dreams or ambitions, where to have nothing happen was a good thing.

For many years I believed that my mother's devotion to being ordinary persisted because she'd come from such an ordinary family. Of course, the truth, as I later learnt, was quite different.

Julie and me in 1955 (I'm in the pram)

Marg Scott (right) having a relaxing cigarette during her tea
break at the Deloraine Aged Care hospital

Russ Scott at Watsonia RSL picnic wearing the
clown suit made by Marg

My first communion—if you look closely, you'll notice a
handkerchief clenched between my praying hands

chapter two

Dreaming big

Unlike my Mother, I wanted more than plain ordinariness.

From a young age I found the notion of having a small life—a little house and a little family in a little suburb—absolutely horrifying, stifling, suffocating. It made me feel panicky and anxious. I hated the idea of ending up leading a life like my mother's—sure, mayhem and madness sometimes surrounded her, but in her own life it seemed to me that nothing ever happened. Apart from finishing a doily she was embroidering, or a dress she was sewing, or having the neatest house in the street, my mother appeared to have no ambitions or goals, and she was avowedly opposed to taking risks, because what if you failed? As for me, nothing was going to stop me in my tireless quest to have an amazing life.

This was by no means an easy ambition to fulfil, given I lived in Greensborough, where, apart from the odd bushfire or murder, nothing much happened. And so began a lifelong habit of pumping up the dullest event, transforming it from the ordinary to the extraordinary—even if it was only inside my own head.

As a young would-be adventurer I was fortunate to be free from the age of five to roam the 'hood, the only rule being that I arrived home in time for tea. To elevate this activity into being amazing I chose to explore the streets on horseback. His name was Raider. The facts that I didn't have a horse and had never ridden one in my life were no obstacle. Of a morning I would set off for school cantering down Adeline Street, holding a dog leash out front, an end in each hand, as the reins. Upon arrival I would dismount and tie the leash to a post, do a few whinnies and head into class.

I didn't always ride. Sometimes I walked. As a child I was quite famous for it. I used to walk 5 kilometres to Eltham to get an ice-cream from the forty flavours shop, such was the lure of an exotic single scoop of black licorice. At other times I threw a broomstick over my shoulder with a nappy tied to the end as a knapsack, Tom Sawyer–style; armed with biscuits and my plastic cordial bottle I'd head to the new housing estate being built in the paddocks of Watsonia to see what adventures could be had—usually none.

Although there was the time my friend Debbie and I had just settled down near a prickle bush (they were common in the paddocks of Watsonia) when suddenly I was grabbed from behind in a headlock.

I couldn't believe it. It was a dream come true. Some real action!

'Hand over the biscuits or I'll belt your friend over the head.'

It was two boys from the state school, and the one who had me by the neck was holding a heavy silver toy gun to my head.

'Don't give him the biscuits, Debbie!' It was an intuitive response. It was as if I just knew how to milk a dramatic situation. Had I simply agreed and said, 'Okay, give them the biscuits,' how dull would it have been? The biscuits would have been handed over and that would have been that. As it was, the whole thing escalated magnificently.

'I said give me the biscuits or your friend is dead.'

Was I really willing to risk my life for a Monte Carlo? No, I wasn't, but I was willing to risk it for the sake of having something extraordinary happen to me. 'Don't do it, Debbie!'

'Give me the biscuit. Or I'm gonna hit her. I mean it.'

Oh, the build-up of tension—it was superb.

Debbie picked up a Monte Carlo …

'No, Debbie, don't!' I cried.

… and she took a bite.

The boys were so taken aback they didn't know what to do, except give me a pathetic little bonk on the head before running away in what appeared to be a state of confusion.

However, while I could be brave by day, when it came to bedtime it was a different story. Oh, how I dreaded that moment when I had to say goodnight. It wasn't fear of being alone; I always shared a room with my sister. The problem was that while everyone else in the house went to sleep I stayed awake, my mind unable to stop creating these dramas that by day were so exciting but by night left me utterly terrified. As a child, every single night—I am not exaggerating—I would cry with fear about something or other.

The communist invasion was a favourite source of terror. I lay in bed listening for the sound of their tanks rolling across the nearby paddocks.

Then there was the fear of dying in a state of sin and consequently burning in hell. (And on that point can I take a moment to thank the nuns for teaching me the concept of eternity when I was four years old.) The thought of being on fire was bad, but the thought of being on fire forever really took fear to a whole new level.

I cried with fear about my parents dying.

The fear about the world ending was especially unpleasant, as it usually involved at the very minimum an earthquake, a volcano, floods and fires, the whole world running around screaming in terror.

I often stayed awake until I heard the *clip-clop*, *clip-clop*, *clip-clop* of the milkman's horse coming up our street in the early hours of the morning. (It wasn't Uncle Frank; he worked in a different part of town.) It signalled to me that all danger had passed, a new day had arrived, and all was well.

It wasn't just adventure and unpredictability that I craved (if only during the day). I also loved an audience. In fact, while my mother worshipped privacy and lived by the mantra 'Don't, whatever you do, draw attention to yourself,' my mantra was 'What's the point of doing anything in life if no-one knows about it?' More than likely this was inherited from my dad and his brothers. From my earliest days I was happiest when in front of a crowd. I loved to sing at family events—no need to ask; I just took the floor.

It appeared that I also had an innate understanding of showbiz principles. For instance, once, at six years of age, I was standing in front of an open fire—specifically, a raging open fire, a *really* raging open fire—performing the classic power ballad 'My grandfather's clock' for all my aunties, uncles and cousins. I was halfway through the song when I realised just how hot my little bare legs were becoming. They were prickling with the heat.

At the three-quarter mark they were scorching.

By the final verse the pain was so intense I was certain I would erupt in flames, but I stayed put and kept going, giving that song everything I had. Why? Because I just knew that, no matter what—death by self-combustion included—The Show Must Go On.

At eight years of age I turned my talents to folk singing and happily took out the Watsonia Community Talent Quest with a rollicking version of 'The fox went out on a chilly night'. I wore a tartan skirt, long white socks and brown school shoes, and won fifty cents and a fountain pen. I was told by the judges that I should have singing lessons. I raced home and told my mother, but she just looked mystified and it was never referred to again. From folk songs I moved on to contemporary hit tunes, and in 1964—I'm not bragging, just stating the facts—my impersonation of Satchmo singing 'Hello, Dolly!' brought the house down in my year four classroom.

Singing wasn't my only way to access an audience. When I was nine—and apologies for this unashamed boast but there is no humble way of expressing such a triumph—I won Miss Junior Watsonia. That's right. I couldn't believe it, either. And, though you may find this hard to credit, until the moment it was announced that 'the winner is Denise Scott' I'd had no idea I was the most beautiful girl in the world.

Admittedly, it was a controversial decision. Mrs Mobilia declared her daughter Tessa would have won 'if only she didn't have a stutter.' She might well have: Tessa was a stunner. But what can I say? On the night in question it was yours truly who took out the title.

I suspect it was my hair that elevated me, quite literally, above the norm. Mum had taken me to Anne Barnes Beauty Salon. Anne herself sported a mauve beehive, and when she'd asked me how I wanted my hair I'd gazed up and without hesitation replied, 'Like yours.'

Anne had weaved her magic, and forty-five minutes later I'd emerged from the salon feeling like a movie star. My shoulder-length, thick blonde hair was piled high on top of my head in a 'do' that was declared by all who beheld it to be 'just like Princess Margaret's.'

The following morning, as I walked down the aisle of St Mary's Church to receive communion, a red sheer-nylon scarf tied under my chin, I felt everyone's eyes upon me and I knew everyone was whispering, 'There's Miss Junior Watsonia. Isn't she beautiful?'

'Denise, 9, poised model,' declared the headline in the local paper the week following the pageant. Underneath was a photo. I was beaming at the camera, wearing a royal-blue sash with gold fringe and holding an enormous cup that my mother and father never did get around to having engraved.

My destiny was obvious—I would become Miss World, no question. It was just a matter of time.

But things didn't go quite according to plan. A month or so after Miss Junior Watsonia I took myself off to the shire hall and entered Miss Junior Diamond Valley. I was completely on my own: no parents, no sibling, no friends. Just me and a dream. Sadly, I didn't get a look-in, didn't even make it to the final forty. I suspect the eczema that had flared up all around my mouth causing the skin to crack and bleed was possibly a little off-putting for the judges.

Having to forsake my dream of becoming Miss World did, however, leave me free to become a missionary and go to Africa and get those wild black savages to put on some trousers and praise God. That was certainly adventurous, if not glamorous, living.

I was forever on the alert, listening to my internal voices, worried that I might miss the Call from God to become a missionary and/or nun. I was pretty keen. Why wouldn't I be? Overseas travel, meeting new people, doing good for mankind, possible martyrdom for my Lord Jesus Christ: it definitely had appeal, and at the very least it wasn't 'ordinary'. But then something happened that changed the course of my life forever.

When I was eleven years old my Uncle Frank invited my mother and me to accompany him to the Comedy Theatre in Russell Street to see British actress Joyce Grenfell in her one-woman show. I had been to a musical before, but that was as far as my experience of theatre went. That night I couldn't believe what I was seeing, or, rather, not seeing. For there was Joyce—tall, thin, elegant and buck toothed—standing all alone onstage, yet I could see children: she was surrounded by them, talking to them, bringing them to life in her famous kindergarten sketches.

Later that night as I lay in my Queen Anne single bed, my glow-in-the-dark Jesus on the Cross gazing down upon me, I prayed with all my heart that God wouldn't call me to become a missionary and/or nun. I now had bigger plans—I wanted to stand alone on an empty stage in a beautiful theatre just like the Comedy and tell stories that I had written.

A proud Miss Junior Watsonia

chapter three

Adolescence

When it came to sex education my mother wasn't too forthcoming. She never mentioned it. Ever.

This meant my sister and I had to scrounge around gathering morsels of information wherever we could until the final piece of the jigsaw fell into place and my sister duly informed me, 'The man puts his dick inside you.'

I was twelve, maybe thirteen, at the time and shocked out of my tiny brain. Why wouldn't I be? Taken out of context it's a repulsive notion. Quite hideous. I'd never even seen a penis. My sister had seen one hanging out of a man's pants in a park while she was on her way to school. She described it as a small, pale-pink sausage. Having a father who delivered smallgoods and having thus grown up surrounded by strass sausages and black puddings, I found that the thought of a small, pale-pink sausage being put inside me did nothing whatsoever to excite.

My introduction to menstruation was an even bigger shock. Mum had never mentioned that, either. I was ten years old, and my sister and I were getting ready for bed when I suddenly screamed, 'Julie, you've cut your bottom! There's blood all over your pants!'

The fact that my twelve-year-old sister had been performing in the school concert earlier that evening and was thus dressed in a white sailor suit made it an even more dramatic and horrifying discovery.

Julie said nothing but headed for the bathroom.

I couldn't believe it. I became hysterical. 'Julie, it's TERRIBLE! You have to tell Mum and Dad. You have to go to hospital.'

'Just shut up.'

My sister never spoke to me like that. What was wrong with her? What had happened? Had she been attacked? Was she too scared to tell anyone? Were her attackers going to come back and kill her if she blabbed?

I didn't know the answer to any of those questions. All I knew was that my sister was bleeding to death before my eyes and I had to do something. Fast.

I raced into my parents' bedroom. Mum had her glasses on. She was reading a magazine. Dad was snoring beside her. I was crying my eyes out. 'Mum, you've got to come, quick. Julie's bottom is bleeding. It's really, really bad. There's blood everywhere and she doesn't want you to know.'

My mother did nothing. Why? Why wasn't she shaking the bejesus out of my father and screaming her lungs out at him to 'wake up, Russ! We have to get Julie to hospital! She's bleeding to death'? All she said was, 'Don't worry about it. It's just one of those things. It's normal. It'll happen to you one day.' And then she went back to reading her magazine.

What the hell? What? *What* was going to happen to me? Was I going to cut my bottom and bleed to death and have no-one do anything about it? Had the entire world gone crazy?

I eventually got an explanation out of my sister, who had had no such knowledge when blood had first appeared on her underpants, and, yes, at the time she had also thought she was dying and was still coming to terms with the shock.

At least I now finally understood what was inside that parcel wrapped in brown paper that my mother always sent me to collect from Mrs Sterndale's newsagency. And it explained those ads—full-page pictures in the *Women's Weekly* that always featured a beautiful model in a dazzling gown standing in a glorious ballroom next to a white Grecian pillar or something equally grand, below which were the words 'Modess … *because.*'

That was it. Not another syllable to be seen.

'What's Modess, Mum?'

'Never you mind.'

Being forewarned, I couldn't wait to get my period, and so when, at fourteen years of age, there was still no sign, I prayed. Now, I'm not saying it was a religious miracle, but I am saying that not too long afterwards I got my first period, at a home mass down the street at the Thomases' house. There was a crowd of us squashed into their tiny lounge room; with the nine Thomas kids plus neighbours there must have been thirty of us. A huge statue of Mary had been borrowed from the local church for the event. The priest stood in front of the TV and conducted the service. Of course, neither of my parents were there.

Later that evening, back at home, I was getting undressed when I saw it—the tiny spot of pale blood on my white cotton underpants. I let out a whoop of joy, threw on my dressing gown and ran into my parents' bedroom. As usual, Mum was reading; Dad was snoring.

'I've got it, Mum! My period! I've finally got it!'

'Good for you.'

I went to my drawer, where a Modess belt and packet of pads had sat in readiness for two years. That night when I was in bed I thanked God for answering my prayer. Who would have thought? My very own version of the stigmata.

It wasn't too long after becoming a woman in the menstrual sense that I got my first boyfriend. His name was Tommy. I was in year nine at Our Lady of Mercy College and was one of the first in my year to have a steady boyfriend.

One lunchtime soon after Tommy and I became an item I found myself all on my Pat Malone in the schoolyard. I was mystified. What the hell was going on? I was usually quite popular. But on this day no-one was coming near me. Everyone was well and truly keeping their distance, staring at me and whispering behind their hands. Well, they weren't really whispering—the word 'slut' was pretty audible.

At first I was shocked. I'd only recently read *The Scarlet Letter* and to be honest most of it had gone right over my head, but my heart did ache for that poor woman being made to walk through the town with the letter 'A' for adulterer pinned to her rags. And now here was I walking around the school being ostracised by my own friends, labelled a slut. However, unlike the woman in *The Scarlet Letter*, I was thrilled to bits about the whole business. I was only just fourteen and had the whole school talking about me. Fancy everyone believing I was capable of any sort of sexual behaviour, yet alone assuming I was a loose hussy.

Even the nuns were swept up in the drama. I went into the year nine cloakroom, where there were two rows of fifty school blazers all squashed together on coat hangers. As I got something out of my bag I heard a noise behind me. I swung around, astonished to see Sister Mary Martha's head pop up from among the blazers. She had obviously been hiding out there, hoping to pounce on whomever she caught in the act of God knows what—smoking or talking dirty or even a bit of lesbian action.

(This wasn't an unrealistic pursuit. After all, there was one out-and-proud lesbian in my year, and she used to play guitar and sing 'I wanna be free', which caused many of the girls to swoon and scream and cry as though she was Davy Jones from The Monkees, and naturally that led some to wonder if they were in love with Davy, who was being channelled through this girl, or with the girl herself, and whether they were therefore lesbian. So many questions at such a young age.)

Sister Mary Martha beckoned me with her finger. 'Is it true you have a boyfriend?'

'Yes, Sister.'

'Is he a nice boy?'

'Yes, Sister.'

'Do your parents know about him?'

'Yes, Sister.'

'Do you kiss?'

'Um, well, yes, Sister, sort of.'

'What sort of kissing?'

'Um, oh, you know, the normal sort … Our lips … touch … sort of.'

'Do you do more than kiss?'

'No, Sister.'

That was true. Tommy had tried to take things further, his hands enthusiastically finding their way into my underpants, but I suspect the fact that I had been wearing a Modess pad the size of a phone book at the time hadn't been quite what he was expecting and he'd quickly abandoned ship.

Not surprisingly, my mother had a very strict policy regarding sex: while her daughters lived under her roof they were not to have it. Not that she ever gave voice to this rule. She couldn't, because in doing so she would have had to come perilously close to talking about sex, possibly even have to say the word. I don't know how I knew this rule; I just did. It was as though I picked it up by means of osmosis, and at that stage of my life I was totally fine with it because I didn't want to have sex. I had no interest in it. This was helped by the fact that I wasn't really attracted to Tommy. I just liked the idea of having a boyfriend.

Weirdly, for such a conservative woman, my mother seemed perfectly cool with the notion of me having a boyfriend. Then again, she didn't know that Tommy's dad was an unemployed, abusive alcoholic and that his mother (so the rumour went) was a prostitute, and that Tommy's seventeen-year-old brother was getting married to his fifteen-year-old girlfriend, who was having his baby. The reason Mum didn't know any of this stuff was because, as already mentioned, she rarely asked questions, so while she never literally rocked back and forth on a chair with her hands over both ears, saying, 'I don't want to know, I don't want to know, I don't want to know,' she certainly had a vibe about her that suggested she really and truly *didn't* want to know.

This 'what you don't know can't hurt you' philosophy proved quite advantageous in my adolescent years.

I didn't know that much about Tommy myself apart from the aforementioned and the fact that he'd left school, worked at the local grocer's and chain-smoked Marlboro cigarettes. I also knew that after seven or so months of 'going together' I was on the verge of dropping him when, lo and behold, Tommy appeared on the front page of our local paper. The headline: 'Boy, 14, shoots at police.'

It was a terrible shock. Tommy had told me he was fifteen.

He and a few friends had stolen a car and fired shots at the police. Tommy got six months in Turana, the youth detention centre. Of course, I couldn't drop him under those circumstances; it would have been too cruel. Besides, now that he was a crim I found him more attractive. In the meantime, if my mum was fazed by any of this, she sure as hell didn't show it.

And so, there I was at fourteen years of age, heading off on my own every Sunday after mass, armed with Marlboro cigarettes and packets of Marella Jubes, on the train to Parkville to visit my man in the clink, like some mini Judy Moran (although admittedly it is hard to picture a *mini* Judy Moran).

During the week we wrote romantic love letters that we'd smuggle to one another across the visitors table. At one stage Tommy even asked me to marry him, but I told him I thought I'd better finish year nine first. Besides, deep down I knew I was more in love with drama than with Tommy.

Brutally, I dropped him two weeks before his release. He broke down and cried, spluttering that he'd never love anyone else as much as he loved me. Yeah, well, whatever, kid. Life was tough and cruel, and the truth was I'd been unfaithful to him.

I'd been to a party and pashed someone else, and to this day I thank God I did, because that person, would you believe—God knows, I hardly can—grew up to be the drummer from AC/DC! I wish there were more to this story, but that's it. I've never seen Phil Rudd since (apart from when he's onstage), but I often retell the story, at dinner parties especially. I like to think Phil does the same.

Of course, at the time of the aforementioned pash I had no idea that Phil (notice I don't use his surname, as though we were, and for that matter still are, best friends) was destined for international fame, but the kissing session with him was significant because I didn't want it to end. I guess what I'm trying to say is—how do I put this delicately?—I felt, shall we say, that Mr Long Way to the Top If You Wanna Rock 'n' Roll made me feel a little bit sexual. And, truth be told, I liked it—so much so, and this is an embarrassing admission, I gave up all 'pleasures of the flesh' activities for Lent. I also gave up choc-mint sundae biscuits—not so much for Jesus but in the hope it would help get rid of the pimples on my chin. It was a long forty days and forty nights in the desert, let me tell you.

Not long after the Tommy business I took a sort of vow. I promised myself—and, for what it was worth, I also promised Jesus—that I wouldn't have sex until I met the man with whom I wanted to spend the rest of my life. It was your basic 'chastity until marriage' vow without the having to get married bit. By the age of fifteen I knew I didn't want to get married— it was way too conservative, too 'normal', too suburban. In other words, it was too much like my mother.

It was 1971, and Eltham had become the place for arty hippie parents and their arty hippie teenage kids. There were mud-brick houses and boys who wore tights and girls who wore headbands, and drugs and sex were all the go. It was all so exotic for a straight-laced Catholic girl from a brick-clad war service home in Greensborough.

At the time, I had a Saturday morning job at Butterworth's Newsagency, where I earnt the princely sum of two dollars. Every Saturday, as soon as I finished work, I headed straight next door to the Indian flea market, one of the first of its kind to open in Melbourne. I was forever putting something on lay-by—a 1940s black jacket with gold bead trim, a 1920s silk shawl with fringing around the edges, and my favourite: a calf-length, red-and-blue embroidered skirt from India. My mother had taught me to embroider as a child, so during those lazy, crazy, hippie, let's-make-love-not-war days, I was able to put that skill to use, embroidering my jeans and t-shirts with mushrooms, gnomes, flowers and peace signs.

My mother rarely commented on Julie's or my clothes, allowing us total freedom to wear pretty much whatever we wanted. The only occasion I recall Mum putting her foot down about an article of clothing was when she banned Julie from wearing a maxi dress that was covered in a swirling, psyche-delic abstract pattern that upon closer inspection revealed naked breasts, including nipples.

Tragically, our mother's lack of fashion policing meant that on more than one occasion I left the house wearing a poncho I had made myself by simply cutting a hole in the middle of a tablecloth and sticking my head through it.

There were also hand-knitted bathers. I kid you not. My mother had taught me to knit as a child, and I was good at it, and for some reason when I was fifteen I chose to spend six months knitting myself a one-piece bathing suit. It was a beau-tiful blue colour with a halter-neck design, in rib stitch, using a fine-ply wool. Without bragging—just stating the facts—I had a great body back then, and the bathers looked fantastic … until they got wet. Who knew wool absorbed so much water and became so heavy? The bathers stretched to the point that the crotch actually hit the ground.

My hair was long, almost to my waist, and blonde, as I've mentioned. Miraculously, it had become blonder since I'd begun using a product called Sun-In. I used to straighten my hair by kneeling down and spreading it out along the ironing board, covering it with a paper bag and ironing it.

As much as I loved the hippie, natural look, being fair haired and of pallid, almost dappled-mauve complexion, my face cried out for assistance in the form of cosmetics. I loved wearing eyeliner, false lashes, a touch of Avon blush stick (purchased from Uncle Frank), white Starlet lipstick and nail polish from Coles.

I was on the cusp of turning sixteen when I met Robbie Buckle. We first set eyes on one another at a dance at Eltham High School. The dance was called Bushbeat, and it was held on the last Friday of every month. It was wild. At that stage of my life it was what I lived for, planned for, continuously fantasised about.

We Catholic girls, with our often ill-deserved reputation for being loose and easy, were more than welcome at the Eltham High dance. There was always a live band playing, including Frame, with its handsome, fresh-faced singer Shirley Strachan, who of course went on to be the frontman for Skyhooks.

We met on the dance floor. I was wearing Lee cords, desert boots and an embroidered t-shirt. Robbie was wearing jeans and an old army shirt and khaki runners purchased from the army disposal store. He was beautiful. He had long, blond, corn-silk hair. (And don't think I'm unaware that 'corn-silk' sounds soppy and pathetic and, well, corny. I just aim to tell things how they are, and corn-silk is the term that springs to mind.) He had extraordinary eyes of a Paul Newman blue. (Note to younger readers: for Paul Newman, substitute Brad Pitt.) And he had dimples. Gorgeous dimples.

Like everyone else we were dancing with a classic hippie attitude, just feeling the music and moving, man, and at some point we jigged into one another's orbit and instead of continuing to jig past one another we hovered on the spot, jigging around one another in some kind of primitive, sexual mating ritual.

(At this point I must take the opportunity, on behalf of all baby boomers, to apologise to all gen Xers and gen Yers and all who come after them. We are so sorry for turning our backs on the waltz, barn dance and Pride of Erin. To think we were the ones responsible for introducing the no-rules, no-partners, completely free-form travesty we dared to call dancing—although, come to think of it, my father had done something similar years earlier. As for hippie dancing, did we think it was attractive? Sexy? Exciting? It may well have been all those things when we were young, but these days go to any sixtieth birthday party and witness a room full of grey-haired, paunch-bellied conservatives jigging to Daddy Cool's 'Eagle Rock' and I defy you to come up with a more tragic image—unless of course it's witnessing the same group 'doing the bus stop'.)

But that night at Bushbeat Robbie and I had no such concerns; we were tearing up the dance floor, our bodies, though at least 10 metres apart, moving as one.

Robbie asked me if I wanted to go outside.

I said yes.

We sat cross-legged on the ground under a gum tree and held hands and gazed into one another's eyes. No, we didn't gaze. We *drowned* in one another's eyes, and that was when I began to fall hopelessly, sickeningly, in big fat love.

And then came another first: an electrifying moment in which time stood still, clocks stopped ticking, my heart stopped beating and birds stopped singing ... (Not that they actually had been singing; it was after all late at night. But had it been dawn they would have ceased chirruping for sure.

Anyway, enough about birdlife. You get the drift.) And then, that exquisite moment when time kick-starts again, and ever so slowly and gracefully and lovingly you head towards one another for that first kiss … Oh, his lips, they looked so soft and tender, and then just as our mouths had touched Robbie turned his head to the side and spewed.

I admit it took me by surprise. I hadn't even realised he was drunk. But I pashed him anyway. Who cared if his mouth was full of vomit? Not me. As the saying goes, 'Love conquers all.' Besides, I didn't know if I'd ever get another chance, so I didn't want to waste the opportunity.

But I did get another chance. Robbie and I became an item, and I often stayed at his house overnight, sleeping in Robbie's single bed while he stayed on the couch in the lounge room. At least, that was what I told my mother, and she went along with it. And to some degree it was the truth. Robbie did stay on the couch until his parents went to bed, and then he would sneak back into his room and crawl into bed with me and … well … nothing.

When I say 'nothing', I mean we did stuff, but we did not have sex.

Ever.

Not only did I remain a virgin; I also managed to remain ignorant of what a penis looked like, a truly remarkable achievement given Robbie's commitment to the task of enlightening me.

God knows, I wanted to have sex with Robbie Buckle. But I wouldn't do it. At the time I told myself I was honouring my vow of chastity to Jesus, but in truth I didn't give that vow any thought whatsoever, because although I was a devoted Catholic I never believed that Jesus was against sex before marriage. I'd always assumed Jesus couldn't care less about sex, especially where, how and when Denise Scott lost her cherry. Why would he be interested? He had so many other things to worry about: African famines, world wars, not to mention the slow and steady march of communism. The real reason I didn't have sex with Robbie was because of my mother's hard and fast rule—it was not allowed to happen while I lived under her roof. I realise plenty of mothers of that generation had that same rule and plenty of their daughters simply ignored it. Not me. I'm not sure exactly what made my mother so powerful. She never raised her voice, never spelt out rules, never threatened us with punishment, and yet we never disobeyed her. It was as though she ruled by stealth.

I suppose I was scared of her.

I consoled myself—or rather kidded myself—that not having sex with Robbie had its advantages. Well, it had one advantage. Robbie had had sex with lots of girls, and I told myself that if I stayed a virgin as opposed to being 'loose' like some of his previous girlfriends his love and respect for me would escalate. It was a risky strategy that failed miserably.

One evening, a couple of months after we had got together, Robbie rang me. Our phone sat on the servery, which meant there was no such thing as a private phone conversation in our house. So when Robbie said, 'Hi, Scotty. I'm just ringin' to let ya know I'm droppin' ya,' all I could say under the circumstances, with my entire family listening in, was, 'Oh, okay, see ya then.'

My heart was broken. I was shattered—sick with sorrow and grief. I stopped wearing make-up. I pulled my long hair back into a tight, unflattering ponytail. And—this may be hard to believe but is absolutely true—I started wearing my school uniform on weekends. It was a horrible sky-blue, knee-length dress guaranteed to bring an adolescent girl's mood right down. I hated wearing it on weekdays, so why, post-break-up, did I start wearing it on the weekends as well? I suppose I was so depressed I was incapable of making a decision about what else to wear. Besides, what was the point? There was no reason to look good any more, no reason to make an effort, no reason to care.

My only consolation was in the evenings, when, as my mother sat under a standard lamp in her armchair, keeping warm by the heat bank (our newly installed modern heating device that was the size of a large dining table), doing her knitting, I sat at her feet, and the two of us had a cup of tea together in our white mugs with red apples painted on them. Night after night we did this. We didn't talk much—certainly not a word was said about my heartache—but still I took great comfort in just being near her, the steady rhythm of her knitting needles a reassuring sound. I guess what I was feeling was loved.

A couple of weeks after Robbie dropped me there was a knock at the front door. It was Robbie and his best friend, Kenny. Robbie grinned. Oh, those dimples. 'So, Scotty, what's with the school uniform?'

Oh my Lord, I felt like such an idiot. It was Saturday. I made up some excuse about having to do a debate. I asked them if they wanted to come inside and wondered if it would be too obvious if I ran to the bathroom and quickly released my hair from its ponytail and put on some mascara.

'No, Scotty, we can't stay, but I just had to see ya, cos …'

He paused; my heart stopped beating.

'… I wanted to see if ya …'

Oh, was he going to ask me out?

'… wanna go out …'

YES. YES. YES. It was all I could do to stop myself from hugging him and screaming.

'… with Kenny.'

With Kenny? It took a few seconds for the words to sink in.

'Kenny wants to take ya to a party, don't ya, Kenny? But he thought it would be weird to ask ya cos of him and me being best friends, but I wanted youse to know I'm absolutely cool with it.'

I looked at Kenny. He appeared to be about to vomit with anxiety. I said that I would go to the party with Kenny. I said this because Kenny looked so stricken with embarrassment.

And so Kenny and I went to the party and had an excruciatingly awkward night that both of us could not wait to be over. I never saw Kenny again.

For that matter, I never saw Robbie Buckle again, either.

Tragically, at sixteen I was still doing calisthenics

chapter four

Kitchen sink surprise

As exciting and dramatic as the crazy rollercoaster ride of young love was, it was a casual conversation at the kitchen sink—a 'Mum washing the dishes, me drying the dishes' scenario—that really got my 'anything out of the ordinary' antennae quivering at that time. I was sixteen years old. I asked my mother what I thought was a simple question. 'Who is that man?'

'What man?'

'That old man we go and see sometimes. You know, the one we call Pa Bock.'

'What do you mean, who is he?'

'I mean, why do we go and see him?'

'He's your grandfather.'

'Is he?'

'Who did you think he was?'

'I don't know. Just some old man we visited.'

I was floored by this news. What floored me even more, though, was the fact I had never bothered to ask my mother about her parents before this. It was so uncharacteristic. I was usually so curious, some might say nosey, especially about family, so why on earth had I never asked, 'Mum, tell me about your mother? And who was your father?' Indeed, here I was at sixteen completely ignorant about my mother's parents. In hindsight it made me wonder if I hadn't, on various occasions, asked my mother some questions about her past only to have her head me off at the pass.

Pa Bock was an old man our family used to visit once or twice a year at his home in Broadford, 90 kilometres north of Melbourne. He was tall, perfectly straight backed and very handsome, with deep-set pale-blue eyes and thick silver-grey hair. He always wore a clean, starched white shirt under a pair of bib-and-brace work overalls, and polished black lace-up leather work boots on his feet.

He'd never behaved like a grandfather or, for that matter, like a father—he'd shown no interest in us and certainly hadn't ever displayed any love or affection towards my mother.

I recalled the one and only time I'd seen him outside his home: I was thirteen and we were gathered at St Mary's, the Catholic church in Tatura. Mum's beloved sister, May, had died suddenly of a heart attack. My mother had gone to Tatura as soon as she got the news. Dad, Julie and I had followed two days later and Mum, upon seeing us, had hugged me in a way I had never known before or since. She enveloped me and squeezed me so tightly that I felt awkward. Who was this emotional woman? Where had my mother gone? At May's funeral I had been even more stunned to see my mother so overcome with grief that my father had to virtually carry her from the church.

Pa Bock had been there, as upright as ever, looking striking in a beautiful old-fashioned—1920s, perhaps?—three-piece grey suit that appeared never to have been worn. It featured a vest with a gold fob watch and chain attached. At the time, everyone had commented on how amazed they were to see Pa Bock there. That night, three years later, as I stood beside my mother at the kitchen sink, it occurred to me to wonder why it had been surprising to see Pa Bock at his own daughter's funeral.

I sensed my mother was somewhat uncomfortable with this discussion, but nevertheless I pushed on with my questions. 'So who is Aunty Peggy, then?'

'Aunty Peggy is Pa Bock's stepdaughter.'

'What? Aunty Peggy is your stepsister?'

'Well, yes.'

Holy Hannah! This was making less and less sense.

Aunty Peggy, as my sister and I called her, lived with Pa Bock. I'd always assumed that she was some sort of live-in housekeeper. She did all the cleaning, cooking, scrubbing and polishing. She waited on Pa Bock hand and foot. She was about sixty when this conversation with my mother was taking place. She had a strong Irish accent, short grey hair, never wore make-up and always dressed in a plain blouse and equally plain skirt that came to just below her knees. She wore black leather lace-up shoes and never wore stockings, only white ankle socks, or bare legs. She had olive skin, and her legs were smooth, naturally hairless (there was no way she would have indulged in anything as modern and vain as hair removal). Her legs were also shapely from her lifetime habit of riding a pushbike, her only means of transport. Neither she nor Pa

Bock could drive a car. There was a good-as-new gig that sat in the back shed, but, since Pa Bock had given up keeping horses long before, it was of little use.

Pa Bock and Aunty Peggy lived in a humble weatherboard house. There were tall pine trees that bordered both sides and meant the sun rarely shone through the windows. Inside, it appeared that time had quite literally stopped somewhere in the 1920s. In the hallway was the original wooden-box wall phone with a crank handle you wound around and around to be connected to the operator; it was their only means of connection to the outside world, not that they connected to it very often. The original wood-fire cooker remained in the kitchen along with a Baltic pine table and matching chairs with kangaroos carved across their backs. There was a formal dining room, where we never sat. Occasionally, I'd sneak in there to admire the elegant dinner gong that sat on an oak sideboard. Unable to control myself, I once struck that gong, an incident that caused Aunty Peggy to come running. 'What on earth? You can't be touchin' that, now. We never use it, except on Christmas Day.' This immediately led me to wonder who on earth would ever have been there to hear it.

In the front of the house was the 'visitors room', where the original 1920s floral lounge suite sat in all its pristine glory, no doubt never having been sat upon. We were certainly never invited into that room; we were always escorted to the lean-to veranda at the back of the house, where the original Coolgardie safe was, the only means of refrigeration. One of Peggy's many jobs was to fill the tray at the top with ice, which then slowly melted, dripping down its sides of hessian cloth.

So disconnected from the outside world was Peggy that in 1970 she asked me, 'What the devil are you talking about? Pantihose? What are they?' And when she clapped eyes upon our first ever family car (as opposed to Dad's work van), a 1962 EK Holden, she almost fainted in awestruck wonder. This may have been appropriate if it had been 1962, but it was 1971, and my dad had bought the car second-hand.

Whenever we visited, rain, hail or shine, we sat in old wicker chairs on the back veranda, which thankfully was enclosed. My dad would put the long-necks of beer he'd brought with him in the Coolgardie. Dad always made sure Peggy got a shandy. He knew the drill. Pa Bock didn't approve of Peggy having beer, so my father would smuggle it to her in the kitchen, where she would keep it out of sight, hidden behind the sugar canister, in case Pa Bock made a sudden appearance.

My mother would always take food to make a meal for everyone. While my mum cooked, Peggy would hover about the kitchen, forever fearful that something might go awry. Tragically, the day arrived when a catastrophe of such horror took place that it became the stuff of legend, forever after talked about at family gatherings—most often referred to as 'the day the custard caught.' For those not familiar with the art of custard making, the custard needs to be constantly monitored while simmering on a low heat. How the custard came to be left unattended on that day no-one ever knew, but my mother and Peggy returned to the kitchen to find the burnt-black saucepan smoking on the stove. So scared was Aunty Peggy of Pa Bock's reaction that she grabbed the pot off the stove, holding it with her apron so as not to burn her hands, took off out the front door at great speed and ran for her life down the street in a crazed, blind panic, eventually hurling the pot behind a bush in a distant vacant block. Showing uncharacteristic feistiness and courage, my mother marched out to the lean-to, squared up to Pa Bock and announced, 'I've just burnt one of your saucepans. I'll buy you a new one tomorrow and post it to you.' And with that she about-faced and returned to the kitchen.

Later that afternoon, on the way home, Mum said, 'Poor Peggy. What a shitful life she must have.' For my mother to swear indicated that Peggy's life must indeed have been very shitful.

I continued my interrogation while Mum continued to wash dishes. 'So who was your mother?'

My mum muttered that her mother was Pa Bock's wife, but she didn't say her name.

'What happened to her?'

'She died when I was two.'

'How?'

'I'm not sure; no-one ever spoke about it.'

'Then who was Peggy's mum?'

'Her name was Bridie. Pa Bock married her not long after Ma Bock died.'

'So what was Bridie like?'

'Not very nice—to me, anyway.'

A year after the kitchen sink surprise, when I was seventeen, Pa Bock passed away, at ninety-two years of age. Aunty Peggy, the sole inheritor of the house, sold it and all the contents at auction. My mother and I went along, more out of curiosity than to buy anything. All the locals had turned out, and there were more than a few excited bargain hunters salivating at the prospect of picking up antiques in mint condition. I was mindlessly looking through a cardboard box of 'sundries'—old cutlery, some Vegemite jars, screws and bolts—when I came across a delicate pale-green glass carafe and matching water glass decorated with hand-painted flowers. It was love at first sight. I wanted it. I showed it to my mother.

'Oh, for goodness sake. I gave that to Peggy for a present years ago—must have been before the war.'

'Can we buy it, Mum? Please? It's beautiful.'

My mother looked decidedly unimpressed. 'Fancy putting that up for auction. It's not as if it's worth anything. I hardly want to pay for something *again* that I gave someone as a gift. How ridiculous.'

After the auction Peggy disappeared, never to be seen again. Rumour had it she returned to Ireland. The carafe and water glass took pride of place on the dressing table next to my bed.

Marg and Russ Scott, 1969

chapter five

Leaving the nest

When I left school I headed off to Melbourne State College to do a teaching diploma. Don't get me wrong: I didn't want to be a teacher. I wanted to be an actress, the dream having stayed with me ever since that night I first saw Joyce Grenfell. Not having any idea how one went about pursuing fame, however, I chose to do a teaching course, specifically, a *drama*-teaching course. Just that word, drama, was enough to get me into a dizzy state of excitement.

In my first year we literally ran around the place dressed in black leotards and tights, feeling the space, feeling the walls and frequently feeling one another. I also studied music, and even though I couldn't play an instrument or read music I managed to get A-plus for a performance of my composition that included a boiling kettle and a choir gargling water. At one point there was a pause in proceedings to allow the audience to listen to the sound of ice melting. Oh, how the music teachers gasped with the originality of it all.

By the end of my first year I was still living at home and consequently still a virgin. As it was during the hippie era this was an extremely embarrassing situation to find myself in. Whenever I got together with girlfriends in the college canteen or the pub and they valiantly tried to recall the names of all the guys they'd slept with I would appear to vague out, staring off into the middle distance, desperate to give the impression I had the same problem—too many lovers, not enough memory. Crazy times!

Being a full-on practising Catholic who still went to church and communion every Sunday didn't exactly sit easily with the free-love, free-spirit, free-thinking hippie scene, either. Not only was it uncool but I'd begun to have serious big-time doubts about Catholicism—many aspects of which now seemed entirely bonkers to me: the Pope's decree that sex before marriage and using contraception were mortal sins, right up there with murder, for instance. What on earth was that about? Who did the Pope think he was? Sure, he was The Pope, but so what? How dare he tell me that if I had sex (not that I had) and used the pill (not that I did) I'd go to hell. How positively insane! (As a Maltese woman declared ten years later, as we lay in neighbouring beds in the Queen Victoria Hospital maternity ward, after having just given birth: 'The day the Pope has my babies for me will be the day I listen to what he has to say about contraception.' Hear, hear sister!)

It also seemed completely bonkers that I was continuing to stick by a religion that my mother had chosen for me but didn't see fit to follow herself. If it wasn't good enough for her then why should it be good enough for me?

But then again the fact was that for so many years I'd been such a big fan of Jesus, loved Him like crazy, so that at one stage I'd even contemplated marriage to Him … not that He'd ever proposed. And there was all the incense burning, and the stained-glass windows featuring images of freshly speared lambs and decapitated heads sitting on serving platters. And, of course, the relatively new ritual of singing folk hymns, the upbeat and jaunty 'Sons of God', being one of my faves.

Since the age of four I'd gone to mass every Sunday, taken communion every week and made regular visits to the confessional—the old 'thinking bad thoughts' being my most consistent sin. How could I just walk away from something that had been so fundamental in shaping my life? The fact was I couldn't do it: I simply didn't have the guts and feared I never would.

At the end of my first year at teachers college I went travelling through New Zealand with my old school friends Anne and Jacinta. We might as well have had neon signs above our heads flashing, 'We are impressionable young women in the process of trying to let go of our Catholic faith and are therefore suckers for anyone offering an alternative.'

Cue the Pentecostals!

We were in a small coastal village on the South Island when we came across an extremely daggy conservative woman playing her guitar and singing songs in praise of the Lord. A fellow traveller, a young guy who was completely strapped for cash, asked if he could borrow her guitar so he could busk.

She replied that she would happily lend him her instrument, on the condition that he only played songs for Jesus.

He replied he couldn't do that because he didn't 'fucking know any.'

She explained that she didn't think music should be used for any other purpose.

That was when I waded in to the debate. Surely music was about being happy and joyful? And surely Jesus would want her to lend her guitar to this young man rather than see him starve to death?

No, she was adamant. Her instrument was only to be used to praise God.

One thing led to another, and the next minute she declared that I was clearly being called by Jesus to join her church. She said that it was the Lord who had brought me to that tiny village in New Zealand. (Weird. I could have sworn it was the chap we'd hitched a lift with.)

Later that night, New Year's Eve 1973 to be precise, while our fellow youth hostellers got drunk and partied on the beach, we were at a Pentecostal meeting in a small wooden hall, waiting to receive the gift of speaking in tongues. At one point, much to Anne and Jacinta's astonishment, I actually began speaking fluent gibberish. But, as I later explained, this was nothing to do with Jesus; rather, it was a drama game we used to play frequently at college.

The girl with the guitar said I was 'fighting The Call,' and so the next evening we found ourselves inside the Pentecostal crusading tent. I was wired, full of nervous anticipation. Was I really about to become a Pentecostal and only listen to songs for Jesus? How could I possibly go through life without Mick Jagger's *Sticky Fingers* or Neil Young's 'Heart of gold', not to mention Melanie's 'Rollerskate song'? And yet there I was. Why? It was obvious I was being called by some higher power;

there could be no other explanation. It was meant to be. It was my destiny.

There was a long table with church leaders sitting on one side while Anne, Jacinta and I sat opposite them. There was candlelight and the mood was solemn as they spoke of their faith and the importance of the Holy Spirit.

With all the strength of a strong ocean tide I could feel myself being pulled further and further towards these people; it was as though I had no willpower to do anything but join them.

And then my friend Anne farted. It was one of those long, quiet farts that go up in pitch towards the end, making it sound like a question. At first, no-one reacted. But then Jacinta, Anne and I got the giggles. We couldn't stop laughing—we became quite hysterical. The Pentecostals were not amused.

Anne did a lot more than break wind that night; she broke the spell of Pentecostalism. It was thanks to that fart that I walked out of the tent and in so doing was saved from having to live life without the Stones. It also inadvertently broke the spell of Catholicism. It gave me confidence: I thought, If I can walk away from the Pentecostals, I can walk away from the Catholics. Sure, it was a much bigger deal but then again, was it? Suddenly it seemed like something that just had to be done. I didn't believe in it any more, and how could I continue to practise something I didn't believe in?

The following week I returned to Australia and never went to Sunday mass again. I was surprised how easy it was. There were no awful consequences—no lightning strikes, no earth-quakes—I wasn't even struck down with sudden inexplicable blindness. And as for Mum? Well, she showed no reaction whatsoever.

During my second year at teachers college I joined an improvisation troupe called Madhat, and we were oh so experimental. Moving to a primitive drum beat we'd go into a 'trance' state and then put on a mask, at which point our teacher would hold a mirror in front of our face and yell 'Flash!' and we'd immediately respond, moving in weird and wonderful ways and speaking total gibberish (it really was all the go at college), having been completely taken over by the spirit of the mask we were wearing.

Early in that year I was sitting in the canteen when a couple of fourth-year chaps came over to my table. I didn't know them but had admired them from afar, having seen them in numerous college theatre shows. They were both exceptionally talented, funny and extremely popular. So why had they chosen to come to my table? I was in a state of swoon when they introduced themselves.

'Hi, I'm Phid.'

'And I'm Mr Right.' (Of course, that wasn't exactly what he said, but for the purposes of my story he shall henceforth be known by that moniker.)

Phid continued, 'We're part of a fourth-year group called D Team.' I knew all about D Team. It was notorious at the college for being the hippie class in which students devised their own curriculum; thus, subjects included bread baking, silk-screen printing for t-shirts, and the formation of a Jimi Hendrix tribute band. 'As part of our fourth-year assessment a group of us are setting up a drop-in centre for street kids. It's in a shopfront in Collingwood. It's a cool place. We've put seagrass matting on the floor, painted the walls, and there's a beautiful open fire …'

Mr Right took over. 'In order to help cover the rent, Phid and I are going to move in upstairs. There are three bedrooms, and we need a third person, and no-one else from D Team is interested, so we were wondering if you wanted to move in with us.'

If I had been in a state of swoon before, I was now in serious danger of fainting. Phid and Mr Right wanted me to move into a drop-in centre with them? I was dizzy with excitement. Coyly, I enquired, 'But why me?'

Phid responded, 'I don't know; you just seem like you'd be crazy enough to want to do something like that.'

I said yes on the spot. No thinking time was needed.

The night I left home, Mr Right came to pick me up in a van he'd borrowed. I'd already fallen in love with him. He was tall, handsome—dark, wavy, shoulder-length hair, beautiful eyes, excellent teeth—funny, a great actor, a marvellous conversationalist, and he could sing and play the sax! But I dared not dream; he already had a girlfriend, and so I contented myself to bask in a delicious feverish, Jane Eyre–state of unrequited love.

As Mr Right helped me move out, my mother sat at the kitchen table, sewing. My sister had married a year earlier, so was already living away from home. My father was out at a footy meeting. We carried my few possessions, including the carafe and water glass, out to the van, while Mum remained fully focussed on her machine. She kept her eyes on the fabric and her foot on the treadle. When it was time to say goodbye she came to the front door and we kissed, just a quick peck on the cheek. Mr Right told her he'd take good care of me, where-upon my heart fluttered and I fell just a tiny bit more in love.

For a young girl desperate to have an amazing, not-so-normal life, the Shop (as it was known) could not have been more per-fect. My upstairs bedroom was literally an extension of the hallway; to get to the bathroom you had to pass through my room. Mr Right and Phid were always very polite.

Knock, knock. 'Sorry, Scotty, but I just need to have a shower. Is that okay?'

Knock, knock. 'Sorry, Scotty, just need to have a piss.'

Knock, knock. 'Sorry, Scotty, I need to clean my teeth.'

Regular visitors from the 'hood included Rodney, Toots, Stretch, Mim and Porky, all between fourteen and seventeen years old. They came to the Shop most nights and hung out in front of the open fire. Wood was never a problem: if we ran out someone would just go and rip a few palings off a neighbour's back fence. Once, I saw Stretch stand up and, cool as a cucum-ber, proceed to smash up the old chair he'd been sitting on and throw it on the flames. Then there was little Arlan, who at the age of seven used to arrive at the Shop on his own every night and stay until 10 pm, at which point we closed up, so I would then have to walk him home and knock loudly on his front door and wait ten minutes or so before anyone answered. Arlan's favourite pastime at the Shop was to kick back on the tie-dye cushions, smoke cigarettes and blow perfect smoke rings with all the worldliness of a middle-aged man.

Police raids were frequent, as were punch-ups, usually a result of local gang rivalry. There were abusive neighbours who wanted us shut down, there was the occasional fire (not in the fireplace but in the backyard, where burning black rubber tyres became a popular activity for a while), and we were once accused of kidnapping a child. No matter how much I tried to explain to the Greek couple from the nearby cake shop that their eight-year-old had come to our drop-in centre of his own accord, they remained hysterical and had the police come and 'rescue' him.

I was in my element!

There was the memorable night that a few of our regulars arrived all pumped up and ready to go and shoot some guy from a rival gang. I was curious. 'Why do you want to shoot him?'

I have never forgotten the answer. 'Because he's a cunt.'

I responded accordingly. 'Well, going on that logic you may as well shoot everyone in this room, because that's exactly what you've called all of us.'

'Yeah, but this guy, he's, well, he's a special sort of cunt.'

Oh yes, for a girl from Greensborough in search of adventure, the Shop was a dream come true.

One night I was sitting in the lounge with a small group of younger kids, including Arlan, when a large, toothless, tattooed male arrived on the premises. He was about my age. 'So, youse a virgin, are ya?' That was Mr Tattooed and Toothless's opening remark. His next remark was, 'I said, youse a virgin, are ya?'

Alright, keep your hat on, handsome, I heard you the first time. (Of course, I didn't actually say that, because, unlike the guy who was asking the question, I wasn't a complete idiot. I knew the situation called for some tact, or who knew where it might lead?) Uncertain what to do, I chose to ignore him and instead kept doing what I was doing—stoking the fire.

Next thing I knew, he had me in a headlock, holding a huge lump of wood above my head. 'I *said*, youse a virgin or aren't ya? If ya don't tell me I'm gonna bash ya.'

I decided to play cool and continued to ignore him.

'Answer the question. Are youse a virgin or not? Answer me or I'll fuckin' bash ya.'

'Yeah, well, go right ahead, cos I'm not going to answer your question.'

'I mean it. I'm gonna fuckin' hit ya.'

'And I mean it. Hit me, cos I'm not going to answer you.'

I learnt something that day—namely, if an angry young man gets you in a headlock and holds a piece of wood above your head and tells you he's going to bash you if you don't tell him whether you're virgin or not and you don't do as he says, it means he's going to bash you.

Gee, it hurt. I actually saw stars. And to think I'd always believed that only happened in cartoons.

Not long after that incident I saw a picture of Mr Tattooed and Toothless in the newspaper. It seemed he'd achieved his dream and had been sent to Pentridge for armed robbery.

And, just to clarify, the answer was yes, I was still a virgin.

While living at the Shop I would ring my mother at least twice a week. I loved chatting to her, keeping her up to speed with all the comings and goings at the Shop. I thought it would do her good to get a bit of insight into the underbelly side of life. And yes, I told her about being hit over the head, although I didn't tell her the reason. It would have been too awkward discussing the 'Are youse a virgin?' question with my mother, sex being the taboo topic it was.

Every week I went home for a visit, no question about it. Regular contact and regular visits with one's parents were a child's responsibility, and so consequently it was always me who rang Mum and me who visited her, rarely the other way around. As with Mum's 'no sex while you live under my roof' rule, her 'keep in weekly contact' rule was never spoken; my sister and I just knew that it was expected. And it wasn't as if it was hard to stick to. I loved my parents' company and I loved Mum's cooking and I loved the fact she did my washing for me. Of course, I would have done it myself, but my mother never allowed my sister or me to touch her washing machine; it was way too precious.

Only once did my parents come to visit me at the Shop, an extremely brave move on their part. I took them into the kitchen. It was only when I went to close the door that I realised it had been kicked in, leaving a huge, gaping hole in the middle. I shut it anyway, to at least give the impression of privacy. As my mother sat drinking tea from a chipped cup I noticed, on the wall behind her, sitting just above her perm, a drawing of a large cock and balls, and beside it a detailed record of all the various dick lengths of our most regular visitors.

Anyway, to cut a long story shortish, over the next few months I began spending more time with Mr Right. Not only were we living together and saving the poor youth of Collingwood, but we were also performing in a musical together. It had been specially written to celebrate the opening of a new, oh-so-modern theatre at college. I was a heroin addict (in the show, not real life). Mr Right was a guru who, at the show's climax, was raised skywards on a cherry picker, at which point I, along with the cast of thousands, gazed up at him, our arms raised in adoration, as we sang, 'Knowing this is the time we've waited for we stand below you gazing in awe …' Suffice to say there was no acting required on my part.

After the show we'd go back to the Shop and, being on a showbiz, adrenalin-charged high, Mr Right and I would lie on his bed and listen to his amazing record collection—the Monterey International Pop Festival, Crosby, Stills & Nash, Boz Scaggs—and we'd talk and laugh and drink freshly brewed coffee. (I never knew it existed until Mr Right introduced me to his Melitta drip filter.) Mr Right still had a girlfriend, a different one from when I first met him. It seemed there was no shortage of interested women, especially since his star turn as a guru. Not that that stopped me dreaming and hoping and being Miss Personality, trying to impress him as I lay on his bed, regaling him with amusing stories, attempting to blow his mind with my intelligence, charm and wit. Alas, at some point in the early morning, Mr Right would inevitably announce that he'd better get some sleep, at which point I'd head back to my room.

But then, one night, approximately six months after moving into the shop, I didn't go back to my room.

A week or so later I went home to my parents' place and shared a roast dinner with them. After the meal, as usual, my mother washed the dishes and I dried. As was customary when standing at the kitchen sink, my mother and I looked straight ahead, never at one another.

As we gazed out into the garden I announced, 'I don't know what's wrong with me, Mum, but when I do a wee it burns like hell.'

Continuing to look straight ahead and without any change to her calm dish-washing rhythm my mother replied in her best no-fuss, low-key voice, 'In our day we called that honeymooners' disease. You need to see a doctor.'

And so, mother and daughter carried on washing and drying the dishes in thoughtful silence.

Mr Right and I became an item, the tricky part being how to tell my parents about our change in status. It wasn't as if I could say, 'Oh, by the way, Mum, Mr Right and I aren't just housemates any more; we're actually having sex,' especially since shacking up with your boyfriend at that time was still considered controversial and in fact referred to as 'living in sin'. I chose to handle it by constantly referring to Mr Right every time I went home for a visit, telling my mother about where we'd been, what we'd done, what we planned to do next.

Eventually, one day when I was standing in my parents' bathroom brushing my hair after having stayed the night, my mother called out from the kitchen, 'So, Denise ...'

'Yes, Mum?'

'Are you and Mr Right ...'

My stomach knotted.

'... going together?'

'Yes, Mum, we are,' I replied.

And that was it. My mother chose to make no comment on the fact that Mr Right and I lived together without being married. If she didn't like it she certainly never mentioned it. Not a word. Indeed, from that moment forth Mr Right was welcome, in fact expected, to attend all Scott-family events. Mum did give me single-bed flannelette sheets for Christmas that year, though. Then again, I did still have a single bed.

(Historical note for younger readers: back in the 1970s, parents did not buy their adolescent child a king, or a queen, or even a double bed for their bedroom at home. Nor did they allow their child's boyfriend or girlfriend to stay in their bed with them overnight—at least, not knowingly. That was why our generation was so keen to move out of home: so we could have sex. And have sex we did; it was just that it was easier, from everyone's point of view, to pretend that we didn't; hence, we kept separate bedrooms and single beds.)

Mr Right and I always slept in his bed. Being a single, it was a cosy situation, but we were in love and, more to the point, extremely slim, and as long as we faced the same way and spooned and didn't ever attempt to turn over, unless of course we both turned at exactly the same time, we were snug and comfortable.

However, 'meet the parents' didn't go quite so smoothly with Mr and Mrs Right Senior. Things got off to a bad start the first time I met them. On the day of the big meet and greet, the plan was to go to Mr Right's family home, be introduced to his folks and then head off together to an extended-family function. I was wearing a long dress. When I say 'dress', it was more like a nightie. Well, it *was* a nightie. It had always been a nightie and always would be a nightie—that is, until it came to a sad and sorry end that night. To give me some credit, it was a lovely nightie, a white cotton vintage affair, the sort of thing a young lass might have worn after a hard day's work on the goldfields. In 1974 those old-fashioned nighties were all the go, in hippie circles at least, the tragedy for me being that Mr Right's parents weren't hippies.

Look, who knows? Maybe the nightie would have won their approval had I not, upon getting out of the car at their house, caught the heel of my shoe in the hem. There followed the most gut-wrenching tearing sound as the fabric across my back ripped, right along the bodice seam. This meant that at the back of my 'dress', the bottom half was no longer attached to the top and now dragged along behind me like a wedding train. Also, the consequent gap between the two halves exposed a great deal of my back, revealing a once-white, now dull-grey bra strap and the top of my equally dull-grey underpants, the elastic of which had long ago lost its joie de vivre.

As luck would have it, Mr Right had a cardigan on the back seat of his car. I put it on and, had it not been for the fact that Mr Right was 6 foot 4 and I was 5 foot 2 and that it was over 35 degrees Celsius that day, it might not have seemed odd that I was wearing an enormous, thick woollen cardigan (whose sleeves, when I stood with my arms by my sides, reached the ground).

Mr Right and I headed towards his parents' house.

I stumbled. 'Oh my God …'

'What now?'

'My shoe …'

'What about your shoe?'

'The sole—it's come completely unstuck. Must have happened when it got caught in my hem. Do you think your parents will have some gaffer tape?'

We were at the bottom of the driveway, and Mr Right's parents were standing on the porch witnessing the entire event. Mr Right took off up the drive. I followed behind, my nightie now not the only thing trailing behind me, because in an attempt to keep the upper and lower parts of my shoe together I was also dragging my foot along the ground.

I made it up the stairs and was introduced to Mr and Mrs Right Senior. Mr Right's dad was friendly enough, but his mother—a tall, good-postured, bespectacled woman—how can I describe the look on her face? Let's just say that had I been a huge, steaming dog turd she'd just stepped on she could not have looked less impressed.

And that was it: the first and consequently last time I ever saw Mr and Mrs Right Senior in a social situation. Given that Mr Right and I were together for some years and he used to visit his parents frequently, this indicated—and hey, this is just a guess—that they quite possibly didn't like me very much.

At the end of that academic year the drop-in centre was closed down and we all moved out. I got the impression our regular visitors weren't too happy about it—perhaps something to do with the way they broke in and destroyed the place. The stairway banisters were ripped out and smashed, windows were broken, cupboard doors were wrenched off hinges, and paint was thrown over the walls. Okay, these youths were angry and disappointed and felt let down, but what were they expecting? That we'd stay?

I felt terrible that I had so capriciously been part of a drop-in centre that, come the end of the academic year, I no longer wanted a bar of. None of us did, so we all abandoned ship and we all felt lousy.

Mr Right, Phid and I moved into a new rental house in Windsor. In order to get the place I'd had to lie to the land-lords, who lived in an adjoining property at the back of the house, telling them that Mr Right and I were married.

It was a lovely big, light-filled house, a perfect place for us to get our lives back on track after the chaos and stress and insanity of living in the Shop. But things didn't go quite to plan. After a couple of months of living in a state of blissed-out domestic happiness, I found my relationship with Mr Right beginning to go awry, big time. Arguments and tears became the norm. As with many love stories, the reasons for our demise were many and unclear, but the fact that his mother disapproved of us living together certainly packed a mighty punch, the pressure proving so great that eventually Mr Right moved out.

On the day that I came home to find Mr Right's bedroom empty I was heartbroken. I'd known it was going to happen but had hoped with all my heart it wouldn't. That night I went to stay with him at his new place—a large, clean, but dreary boarding house where everyone had their own bedroom with a locked door. Mr Right's room was on the second floor.

The following morning he went to work. I was still in bed dozing when suddenly I woke in fright. I heard a key in the door and watched it slowly open.

I whimpered Mr Right's name. 'Is that you?' No-one answered.

An old lady's head appeared around the door.

We both gasped in fright.

She walked into the room. She had a bucket in one hand and a mop in the other. She informed me she was the cleaner and said didn't I know that 'the men who live in this boarding house are not meant to have ladies stay the night?'

I wanted to explain that I wasn't just any lady; I was Mr Right's wife—sort of—but of course I wasn't Mr Right's wife, so I said nothing.

'I'll give you two minutes to get out or I'll call the landlord, and then your friend won't have anywhere to live, will he?'

She left the room.

I got out of bed, pulled on my clothes and headed into the hallway, past the cleaning lady, who, mop and bucket in hand, stood looking at me as though I was scum. Or maybe she wasn't looking at me that way. Maybe it was just that I saw myself in that light.

I started to descend the stairs, but halfway down all of a sudden I couldn't breathe. I gripped the banister. I desperately gulped for air but couldn't seem to get any into my lungs. Not having had an attack for years, I had assumed I'd grown out of asthma.

I eventually got down the stairs and across the road to a tram stop. There was a kindly man there who assisted me onto the tram. I struggled for breath, and people offered to call an ambulance, but I stayed on the tram and managed to get myself to the student doctor at college.

After writing out a script for medication the doctor suggested I go home and get some rest. And at that moment, there and then in the doctor's surgery, I started weeping and couldn't stop—good for me, terrible shame for the doctor. He had a lot of people waiting to see him. I explained to the doctor I couldn't go home; I hated the thought. It felt too lonely.

The doctor suggested that perhaps I could go to my parents' place.

Much to his dismay I wept even more, explaining that my parents didn't know anything about this mess and I didn't want them to find out.

'What about friends? Do you have a friend you could go and stay with?'

'I don't want my friends to know about any of this either … I just want to be with my boyfriend.'

I went on to explain that even if there had been somewhere for me to go I couldn't, because I had to be at a rehearsal in less than two hours. And it wasn't just any rehearsal: it was the final dress rehearsal for a show that was premiering that night—a loosely scripted piece put together by Madhat based on the medieval redemption play *Everyman*. I was playing the role of a leper. I could not have felt more suited to a role. Not that it was me exactly playing the part; it was a puppet I had made. His name was Simon and he only had three fingers on each hand—hence his suitability for the leper gig. We'd spent months creating the show, and this performance was a big deal: lots of showbiz and arts-funding people were invited and in two days' time we were heading off on a state-wide tour.

To my amazement the doctor asked his receptionist to make me a cup of tea, and then he took me into the next room, a doctor's surgery that wasn't being used at that time. He gave me a pillow and a blanket and suggested I try to have a rest. What a good and great man!

That night the theatre was abuzz with all the razzle-dazzle excitement of a Broadway opening. Before the show I stood in the foyer waiting for Mr Right, who had promised to meet me there. I longed to tell him about my day.

I waited.

He didn't show.

I told myself he was most likely caught in traffic.

Feeling vulnerable and still struggling to breathe properly, I made it through the first half of the show, grateful to be standing behind a puppet whose performance as a leper was, it has to be said, wowing the crowd.

During the interval a message arrived that Mr Right was sorry but he couldn't make it to the show; he'd decided to play basketball instead, and he'd be in touch.

My heart, which had been on the verge all day, finally broke.

The second half of the show went ahead without me, with the director forced to take over Simon. I simply could not stop crying; nor could I breathe very well.

A lecturer from college kindly offered to drive me home to my parents' place in Greensborough. I arrived on their door-step and knocked on the front door.

My mother opened it. 'Denise, what's wrong?'

I couldn't speak. I couldn't begin to explain. I just stood there and wept.

My dad appeared and stood behind her. They thanked the college lecturer for caring for me, and soon I was sitting at their kitchen table, drinking a freshly made cup of tea and eating Savoy biscuits and cheese.

At one point, Dad stood up. 'Well, I'll leave you girls to it,' he said, assuming that it was a mother–daughter discussion that was in order, and so he headed for bed. But I told my mother nothing. I couldn't tell her my troubles—we'd never done that sort of thing, and I certainly wasn't about to start. How dreadfully awkward would that have been? And so I contented myself instead to simply sit there and drink tea with her.

The next morning, Mum accompanied me to the family doctor, the same one I used to go to as a child. She even came into the doctor's office and sat with me. He examined me and announced I was in a very weakened state. The asthma was serious and my immune system was low; I needed to down tools, stop everything and rest for two weeks minimum.

I explained that I couldn't do that, because the next day I was embarking on a theatre tour.

'If you go away on that tour, you'll come back in a coffin.'

My mother and I sat there staring at the doctor. Surely he was being a little overdramatic?

He assured us he wasn't. Did I understand how sick I was?

'Yes, but …' I decided not to finish the sentence. I somehow doubted the doctor would agree with the sentiment 'the show must go on.'

The next morning, at some ungodly hour, my father drove me in his sausage van to Carlton, where I boarded the minibus and headed off on the Madhat tour. My mother had farewelled me with what came close to being a hug.

We performed in small country towns all over regional Victoria to audiences of fourteen people (on a good night). Apparently, medieval miracle plays performed by actors speaking gibberish while in a trance state wearing papier-mache noses were not hot-ticket items at that time. But the play had a healing effect on me. I enjoyed being away from Melbourne, being on the road with Madhat, sharing a motel room with the actress who played Mary Magdalene. She was great company, and I so preferred it to being alone.

My health improved to the point that one night I got drunk. 'Jesus' and I stayed up late and drank a flagon of cheap port between us. I have never been able to drink it since. About three-quarters of the way through the flagon, 'Jesus', who assumed Mr Right and I were surely on the brink of breaking up, looked at me with his beautiful dark, deep eyes (he had glorious olive skin as well—hence him being cast as Jesus) and told me he was in love with me and had been for some time.

You could have knocked me over with a feather, and not just because by that stage I was approaching alcoholic poisoning. I had had no idea this love existed, and I found it incomprehensible that of all the men I knew it was the terribly handsome, kinder than kind, extraordinarily talented 'Jesus' who was in love with me—the sickly, wheezing, sadder than sad leper.

I didn't muck around. Responding with a straightforward—possibly bordering on brutal—honesty I informed 'Jesus' that there was no point in him loving me. It could never be reciprocated, as I loved Mr Right and intended to do so for the rest of my life, and that, my Lord Almighty, was that.

The next night, as 'Jesus' hung from the cross in a small wooden hall in Ararat, crying out, 'My God, my God, why hast thou forsaken me?' I sensed a little more emotional anguish than normal.

In my final year at teachers college I was still in a relationship, albeit an oft-times rocky one, with Mr Right, who remained in the boarding house while I continued to live in the share house in Windsor, having told the landlords, 'Sadly, my marriage is in trouble and my husband has left me.'

During the year I celebrated my twenty-first birthday. I didn't want a party—it was way too 'conservative establishment' for me. But my parents wouldn't hear of not having one and decided that, since it was also my grandfather's eightieth and my Aunty Edna and Uncle Fred's silver wedding anniversary around the same time, they would combine all three events and have a celebratory Scott-family gathering in our aluminium garage.

And I'm glad it went ahead. I still use the CorningWare casserole dish that one of my aunts gave me; and as for the heavy silver bottle-top opener featuring a glass knob on the end inside which is a pink flower—a gift from my uncle and aunt's bridesmaid—it sits inside a drawer still in its original crimson-velvet-lined box, waiting for that moment when it will finally come into its own and be of some use.

It was a great party. My cool and groovy drama friends from teachers college had never seen anything quite like it— especially when Uncle Ken began bashing himself over the head with the scone tray and my father appeared in his clown suit. My mother did all the catering, and to this day my friends still rave about her homemade sausage rolls.

I was now in D Team at teachers college and had chosen to do an elective in bicycle riding. (Disappointingly, the 'How to grow and use wheatgrass' class had been full.) As part of my assessment I had to go on a 40-kilometre bike ride, an extremely adventurous move on my part. Not only did I not own a bike, but I didn't know how to ride one.

One weekend before the bike ride I went with my parents to stay at Cousin Nor's house in Shepparton. It was her fiftieth birthday. That Sunday afternoon, Noreen's sons dragged an old two-wheeler bike out of their shed, dusted it down and helped me climb on board, and by 5 pm there I was, at twenty-one years of age, riding around Noreen's Hills hoist screaming, 'Mum! Dad! Look at me! Look at me! I'm riding a bike! I'm riding a —' and that was when I fell off and felt quite foolish, given that everyone had come running outside to witness the historic event.

Back in Melbourne I bought myself a fancy bright-green ten-speed bike, and five days later I arrived at the starting point for the 40-kilometre ride.

The leader of the expedition asked if anyone was inexperienced. I was the only one to put up my hand and was assigned a 'guide'. His name was Jim—he was a ring-in, a friend of a fellow D teamer—and he explained he would 'shadow' me for the entire journey.

And so off we set. The first few kilometres were a breeze. The road was flat and straight—so much so that at one point I even managed to ungrit my teeth and smile, but only briefly, because the next thing I knew we were going up a steep hill.

I was struggling when Jim rode up beside me. 'Scotty, why don't you change gear?'

I didn't answer. Not because I was being rude, but because I didn't have any breath to spare on verbalising words, plus I felt too humiliated to admit I didn't know how to change gear. I'd never done it before, and besides, it required me to take my right hand off the handle bar, and I was terrified by that thought.

At this stage, the climb was so steep that my bike was wobbling, having almost come to a standstill.

'Scotty, why won't you change gear?'

I felt trapped and told Jim the truth.

With no fuss or fanfare he moved in close, leant across and changed my gear for me, and that night I slept with him.

The fact that I had only ever slept with one man before, not to mention that at the end of that 40-kilometre bike ride I couldn't walk, indicates the true magnitude and charm of the man. Then again, the fact that at the end of that 40-kilometre bike ride I also couldn't close my legs possibly made the task that much easier. Or perhaps it was indicative that I was finally ready to move on from Mr Right?

Except I wasn't ready to move on; I wanted to stay with Mr Right.

So why did I sleep with Jim?

The answer is simple. Although 'simple' may be an exaggeration. I slept with Jim because Mr Right had slept with other women before he met me and, for that matter, possibly while he was with me. I had my reasons for being suspicious, including having been at a party during which I walked into a bedroom to find him pashing one of my 'friends'; and then there had been that note I found in his bedroom from a stunning young blonde 'friend' of his. She had done a drawing of an open fire and 'just wanted to say thank you for the beautiful night we shared together.' It did make me wonder. And to make matters worse she rode a Harley. (How could I, a woman who couldn't even ride a pushbike, begin to compete?) Anyway, Mr Right's possible indiscretions aside, I had always fancied, hoped, aimed to be a bad-ass-mamma type myself—wild, reckless, unpredictable, sexy—but here I was having slept with only one man. It just wasn't good enough!

But why Jim? The answer is as ancient as time. I slept with Jim because he was attractive and he made me feel good about myself. Even though I couldn't change gear he still wanted to have sex with me.

I soon learnt that Jim wanted to have sex with most women. He loved women—all women. Young, old; skinny, fat; brunettes, blondes, red heads; short haired, long haired, bald; one legged: you name her, Jim loved her, especially if she happened to be in a not-so-happy relationship and he could set about rescuing her, liberating her, making her see once and for all that she deserved better. That he was an ex-sailor who'd spent many years roaming the world with the navy, eventually jumping ship in Australia, where he became a dope-smoking hippie electrician who played the flute, proved to be a heady mix for the ladies, especially the more vulnerable among us, and so suffice to say Jim was a busy boy.

Almost immediately, I informed Mr Right about my involvement with Jim the Hippie and got the impression (and perhaps I was kidding myself) that he was okay with it. I suppose he didn't have much choice. Perhaps he was too busy riding Miss Harley-Davidson in front of the open fire in his bedroom to care.

I loved hanging out with Jim the Hippie. We went for bike rides, long walks and even a camping trip with a tiny igloo tent—a marvellous design that didn't need pegs. (However, it did need people inside it to keep it on the ground. Sadly, we found this out on the first morning of our trip when we crawled out only to have a gust of wind come along, pick up our igloo and blow it into the river, where the current swept it away like a large beach ball, never to be seen again.)

But, as fun as Jim the Hippie was, I soon realised I wasn't in love with him, and, as much as I wanted to be a crazy, unconventional wild child, the truth was I couldn't have sex with someone if I didn't love them. So Jim the Hippie and I stopped being lovers—no hard feelings—and remained friends. I returned to being the monogamous and loving partner of Mr Right.

But not for long.

My home in Teddywaddy West, Wooroonook Road

chapter six

Teddywaddy dreaming

I was at my parents' house when I opened the letter from the Education Department informing me I was being sent to teach at Wycheproof Education Centre. Immediately, I burst into tears and threw what could only be described as a tantrum. This display of unbridled emotion was a rare event in Adeline Street, and my mother told me to pull myself together. 'For goodness sake, Denise, it's not that bad.'

'Not that bad? Easy for you to say; you're not the one who has to live there!' And with that I ran sobbing from the house. It was the closest my mother and I had ever come to 'having words'.

Not only did I not want to go to Wycheproof, but I didn't want to teach. I wanted to be an actress! That was the only reason I'd gone to teachers college, but now, here I was, legally bound (I'd been on a government studentship) to teach for at least three years in a wheat-farming town 300 kilometres north of Melbourne.

To my surprise and delight I fell in love with Wycheproof. I loved the red dust. I loved the pale-yellow fields of wheat. I loved the huge, gnarled, dappled-grey gum trees and the soft, silver light that made everything shimmer at sunset. I loved my work colleagues. I loved the kids I taught. I loved being invited to their homes to share an evening meal with their family—typically a three-course affair consisting of soup, roast and dessert and followed by a huge homemade passionfruit sponge.

More than anything, I loved discovering that beneath the surface of this seemingly sleepy, uneventful, boring town where—apart from mouse plagues, wheat business and the annual amateur musical production—nothing seemed to happen, there beat a wild, passionate, crazy heart. Life was far from 'ordinary'. There were teacher–student relationships and closeted homosexual activity. And there was the scandalous behaviour of an unlicensed teacher driving a carload of students home to their billets while away at a school sports competition. (I had no choice. The physical education teacher had sprained his ankle and was on crutches and couldn't drive, and, oh yes, he was also quite drunk. His car was an automatic, though, which was just as well considering I had never driven before in my entire life; and one of the students knew what to do so they were able to instruct me.)

The only thing I didn't like was living so far out of town. I was renting an isolated farmhouse about 12 kilometres from the school, postal address Wooroonook Road, Teddywaddy West, via Wycheproof. It wasn't the fact that I had to ride my pushbike to and from the school; I loved that. It was the loneliness. In theory I shared the house with another teacher, but in practice she always stayed over at her boyfriend's place in town, leaving her large, crazy black dog, Ninja, with me at the farm-house. Perhaps it was because his owner was never there and I had no experience caring for a dog, but, whatever the reason, Ninja was extremely mentally unwell. He tore everything to shreds (including my washing). He killed local livestock. He leapt on people and nipped at their faces. What I'm trying to say is that Ninja was not very good company.

Given my penchant for insomnia, paranoid thoughts and a basic fear of the dark, night time was never my best friend. This was especially so in the wilds of Teddywaddy, where, as a young woman living alone in an isolated farmhouse without a car or, for that matter, a licence to drive one, I would lie in bed listening for the sound of heavy boots *click-clacking* along the return veranda, making its old wooden slats creak. Or maybe it was the boots creaking? Who cared what was creaking; all I knew was that there were footsteps, and every single time I heard them, which was every single morning at around 2 am, I was paralysed with fear. I tried to reassure myself that it was just a friendly ghost. (It had to be, right? I mean, it hadn't hurt me thus far, had it? In fact, could ghosts actually hurt people, or did they just send them crazy with fear?) Eventually, the footsteps would disappear, the *creak-creak-creaking* gradually fading into the dusty, barren, distant paddock.

Then there was the time a ute full of men firing guns came screaming down my driveway. If you could die from fear I most certainly would have died that night. I hid in the cellar, located through a trapdoor underneath my kitchen table. I sat there in the dark, fully expecting the trapdoor to be opened and my gun-toting visitors to murder me. The next day, having emerged from my Anne Frank hideout, I learnt they were pissed locals who'd come to shoot some rabbits.

There was also an incident with the geography inspector. Back in those days school inspectors roamed the state, their job being to sit at the back of classrooms and assess teachers' performance. This particular inspector was your typical Education Department chap, slightly balding on top, dressed in an ill-fitting suit, his shirt just a little too tight across his small paunch, and dusty, unpolished shoes. By day he was friendly enough, and come the end of his visit I happily joined him and a few other teachers at the pub for dinner and drinks. The inspector was staying the night with John and Dave—fellow schoolteachers who also happened to be my nearest neighbours—and, since their house was just 2 kilometres further along the Wooroonook Road from mine, he offered to give me a lift home. I accepted.

We were driving along Wooroonook Road, and as far as I knew all was well with the world, when completely out of the blue Mr Geography Inspector suggested we have sex.

I politely refused, and that was when I became uneasy and a teeny bit scared. I wasn't sure why—it was just a vibe he was giving off—that and the way his eyes had gone all squinty and he'd started sweating and breathing heavily and glaring at me and muttering to himself under his breath.

Not wanting him to come up my long and lonely driveway, I asked him to drop me off at my front gate.

He obliged and zoomed off, leaving a cloud of angry red dust in his wake.

I was about halfway up the drive when I heard the roar of a car engine. I looked over my shoulder and saw headlights approaching, and quickly. Mr Geography Inspector had turned round and was coming back for me!

The car turned into my driveway and sped up it.

I took off and ran into the paddock in front of my house. To my dismay Mr Geography Inspector followed, his car jumping and bumping across the rutted field while I stumbled and scrambled and only just managed to stay upright. Once or twice I dared to look back over my shoulder, only to be dazzled by the headlights.

And then, into this *Wake in Fright* nightmare lurched Ninja, flying through the air …

Oh, bless you, beautiful boy, coming to save me! And to think I'd spoken of you so poorly.

… and then he started attacking me.

Ninja, what the hell? You stupid dog. I'm your friend; I live here.

But with the deranged geography inspector still zooming towards me there was no time for dog whispering.

And so, with two crazy animals now chasing me, I ran like I'd never run, and eventually I made it onto my front porch and into the house. Mr Geography Inspector sped back off into the night, never to be seen again. Ninja resumed chasing rabbits.

And to think, when I'd first heard I was being sent to Wycheproof, I'd sobbed to my parents, 'But what will I *do* there? It's going to be so dull!'

More often than not, of a weekend I returned to Melbourne and stayed with Mr Right. But on one memorable occasion I remained at the farmhouse. It was late on Friday afternoon when the phone rang. It was Jim the Hippie. He explained he had been staying in a nearby town, having gone to fix some wiring for a 'friend'. (I interpreted this to mean he was having an affair with a lonely farmer's wife whose husband had gone away for a few days.) Jim the Hippie was considering hitching over to my place that night so we could catch up. (I interpreted this to mean the husband was making his return a day or so earlier than expected.) He wanted to know if it would be okay if he stayed at my place for the night.

I said it would be fine.

He asked directions.

I said they were complicated—best he get a lift into Wycheproof and then ring me and I'd organise for someone to pick him up and bring him out to the farmhouse.

In order to fully appreciate the ensuing drama, one has to understand that not only did mobile phones not exist back then but my home phone went via the local telephone exchange. Every time I picked up the receiver I immediately spoke to an operator. The reverse was also true: every time someone called me they went via an operator.

As soon as I hung up the phone I began to worry about Mr Right and how he would feel about Jim the Hippie coming to stay with me. Not that any shenanigans were going to happen—I was well and truly over Jim and vice versa—but nevertheless it didn't feel right. And so I decided to ring Mr Right to tell him what was happening.

I picked up the phone.

'Hello, Teddywaddy West two-one-three. What number, please?'

I told the nasal-voiced operator Mr Right's number. She put the call through.

His housemate Trev answered.

I asked him if Mr Right was home.

'No, Scotty, he's already left.'

'What do you mean, he's already left?'

'I mean, he's already left to go to Wycheproof. Didn't he tell you?'

'No …'

'Oh shit, he must be wanting to surprise you. Sorry, Scotty.'

'When did he leave?' I tried to sound nonchalant.

'He must have left an hour ago, maybe an hour and a half.'

I almost fainted. My heart started pounding, and beads of guilty, panic-fuelled sweat formed on my furrowed brow. (That's not true. I never sweat, not even in times of crisis. But the image does go some way to conveying how anxious I was.) Jim the Hippie was on his way! And now Mr Right was also on his way! What if they arrived at the same time? Mr Right would think Jim the Hippie and I had planned a clandestine rendezvous!

Oh my God, this was a disaster. Oh God, oh God, oh God. I reminded myself to breathe. Then I did a quick calculation. If Mr Right had left Melbourne an hour and a half earlier, there was another hour and a half before he would arrive. As for Jim the Hippie, I didn't know how long it would take him to hitch to my place. But both men were on the road heading towards Teddywaddy West from opposite directions. At all costs I had to prevent them from meeting.

There was no time to lose. I formulated a plan and immediately put it into action. Firstly, I rang my friend Jane. She taught at the school with me and lived in town, near the main street. She agreed that Jim the Hippie could stay at her place for the night. When Jim rang me I would give him Jane's phone number and they could arrange to meet.

But hang on, what if Jim the Hippie rang my place and Mr Right had already arrived? My phone was attached to the wall in the hallway. There was no hope of a private conversation. How would I be able to tell Jim about going to stay with Jane without Mr Right overhearing and becoming suspicious? Alright, okay, I had to find some other way of communicating the change of plans to Jim.

I went to the phone and lifted the receiver.

'Hello, Teddywaddy West two-one-three. What number, please?'

'Um … hello. Yes. Well, you see, I don't actually want to be connected to anyone. I was wondering if you could do me a favour …'

The operator said nothing.

I pushed on regardless. 'You see, I have this friend who is on his way to Wycheproof and he was going to ring me when he arrived in town, but my plans have changed and I was wondering, when he does ring, if instead of putting the call through you could give him a message?'

'What message would you like me to pass on?'

'Well, his name is Jim, and could you please tell him that my boyfriend is now coming for the weekend, so he can't come to stay with me, and he has to ring my friend Jane Thomas. Her number is —'

'Two-one-seven. I know Miss Thomas. She teaches my kids English. Actually, you teach one of them drama.'

'Oh really?' I laughed, admittedly without any sense of amusement.

I hung up the phone. To be sure, it was an awkward situation. But I told myself that even if the whole town was talking about the crazy drama teacher the following day, I didn't care. As long as Mr Right and I were all hunky-dory, being the cause of country-town gossip was but a small price to pay.

I changed my clothes and put on some make-up in readiness for my man's arrival. I heard a car coming up the long driveway. It was Dave and John. They were on their way to the pub in town for a meal. Did I want to join them? I decided I might as well. There was still at least an hour until Mr Right arrived. It would provide a good distraction. I left a note on the kitchen table in case Mr Right turned up while I was out, explaining I was at the pub and telling him to meet me there.

It was 8 pm by the time we finished our meal. Mr Right hadn't shown up at the pub. As it was now well over three hours since it was rumoured he had left Melbourne, he should have arrived.

I went to the phone box in the main street, rang the operator and asked to be put through to my farmhouse. The phone rang out. Where was he? Maybe his car had broken down. Maybe he'd been held up somewhere. Maybe he'd tried to ring me …

Oh shit. Oh fucking hell. Please, God, no.

Once more I picked up the receiver.

'What number, please?'

'Hello, it's me again, Denise, the drama teacher, from Teddywaddy West two-one-three. You just put me through to my house and no-one was there and, well, I was just wondering, has anybody tried to ring me?'

'No, Denise, no-one has.'

Oh, the relief. This meant Mr Right hadn't rung and inadvertently been given the message meant for Jim the Hippie—namely, not to come to the house because Denise's boyfriend was on his way. What would Mr Right have made of such a message?

I took the opportunity to avert such a mishap by giving further instructions to the operator. 'There may be another man who tries to ring me …' I told her Mr Right's name, 'and it's very important that he doesn't get the message meant for Jim.'

'I see. So let me get this clear. If your friend Jim rings I tell him your boyfriend is on his way and not to go to your house, and if your boyfriend rings I tell him … what?'

'That I'm at the pub but will be home soon.'

It was 9.30 pm when Dave and John dropped me back at the farmhouse. Still Mr Right was a no-show. Once more I rang the operator. Before I said anything she informed me that neither Jim nor my boyfriend had rung. I thanked her and told her to forget about passing on any messages; I could no longer cope with the tension. I had bigger concerns: I was worried sick about Mr Right. Again I asked the operator to put me through to Mr Right's home phone, and again his housemate answered. I told him Mr Right hadn't arrived. 'Are you sure he left Melbourne around four-thirty?'

'Absolutely certain.'

By 11 pm I was convinced Mr Right had been involved in a car accident. I rang the operator. A different voice answered. He sounded young. I asked to be connected to Mr Right's house. This time no-one answered. Trev must have gone out.

And so I waited.

That darned farmhouse—so far away from anywhere.

I rang the operator again. This time I didn't ask to be connected to anyone. It was nearly 1 am; who could I ring at that hour? It was the operator I wanted to speak to. I asked him if he had heard about any accidents on the Hume Highway.

He said he hadn't.

I explained why I was worried.

He listened and sympathised and offered to ring the police and check with them. He promised he'd ring me back straightaway. He did exactly that, informing me the police had received no reports of car accidents. He told me to ring him any time during the night, that he was there to help.

I made myself a cup of tea and turned on the radio. The reception was bad, but it was better than the silence.

An hour later the phone rang. My stomach lurched. Mr Right?

It was the operator.

'Have you heard something?'

'No, Denise, I haven't. I was ringing to see how you were going.'

What a kind and thoughtful young man. The truth was I wasn't going too well. Being in the farmhouse on my own in the middle of the night was doing nothing to quell my fear that Mr Right was lying dead somewhere.

And what of Jim the Hippie? I hadn't given him a thought for hours, because I wasn't in the least worried about him. My instinct told me he'd more than likely been picked up by some bored, sexually frustrated country woman who at that very moment in time was giving Jim a ride, in more ways than one.

Of course, I didn't tell the young operator any of this, but I did tell him about the ghost that haunted my house.

He interrupted me, saying he'd have to hang up as there was a call coming through.

He rang back immediately and said he was sorry but it hadn't been Mr Right.

I burst into tears.

The operator calmed me. He assured me he was there for me, that I could ring him any time.

And I did.

And he rang me.

And, each time, we talked and talked. He asked me about my life. Where had I grown up? What brought me to the country? How did I meet Mr Right? How long had we been together? In turn I asked him about his life, not that I paid attention to his answers. I was too distracted, fantasising about what I'd wear to Mr Right's funeral—definitely black, maybe even a lace mantilla—and how I would assert my right to sit in the front seat at the church even though I knew his parents would be against it.

I stayed awake the whole night, didn't doze off for one second. At 7 am I was once more connected to Mr Right's home phone. Trev—his bleary voice indicating a hangover—answered. I was sobbing uncontrollably. I told him Mr Right hadn't arrived, that I didn't have a clue where he was.

I rang Mr Right's boss, apologised for waking him so early on a Saturday morning, and asked if he had any idea where Mr Right could be. All he could tell me was that when Mr Right had left work the previous afternoon he'd told everyone he was heading to Wycheproof.

I rang Mr Right's friends. They all said the same thing: that as far as they knew he'd been heading to Wycheproof to spend the weekend with me.

I rang my parents and wept. My mother told me she was sure everything was fine, but even she didn't sound convinced.

It was now 9 am, and everyone in Melbourne who knew Mr Right was on the case, trying to track him down. In the meantime, the young phone operator finished his shift. I thanked him for his kindness.

At midday the phone rang. It was Mr Right, as bright and breezy and upbeat as you like. He was ringing from my parents' house. He'd been playing basketball nearby and called in to see them.

'Where have you been? I thought you were dead. I've been awake all night. You told everyone you were coming to Wycheproof. You weren't at your place, so where were you? What happened?'

He couldn't explain how everyone had got the impression he was going to Wycheproof. Obviously, there had been a misunderstanding, because what he had done was go away with a couple of his blokey mates to a beach house down the coast.

Oh, the sweet relief!

Jim (have I mentioned he was a hippie?) arrived at the farmhouse later that afternoon, having spent the entire night sitting by the side of the road unable to get a lift. We were both physically and emotionally wrecked. I showed him the spare bed, and I headed for mine, and we both slept for hours.

A few weeks later, I heard there had been an accident at a notorious railway crossing nearby—a young man had died at the scene. He had worked at the local telephone exchange.

Months later, during some sort of emotional breakdown confession, Mr Right admitted to me that, while he *had* gone to a beach house that weekend, he had *not* been with his blokey mates. He'd gone away with a sexy work colleague and her equally sexy friend for a ménage à trois.

Well.

One hot and dusty Sunday afternoon in 1977, Fleetwood Mac, Santana, Billy Thorpe and Little River Band played a concert at Calder Park Raceway, on the outskirts of Melbourne. I was in town for the weekend, staying with Mr Right, and we went to the concert together. The plan was that after the concert I would head back to Wycheproof on a large tour bus full of locals who were also at the show.

At the end of the night, before bidding each other farewell, Mr Right and I partook of a joint. I wasn't used to smoking dope, and this perhaps explains the tremendous sense of peace and happiness I experienced. I could not have been more relaxed as I stood by the side of the highway at about 6 pm and waved goodbye to Mr Right, watching him head off down the Calder Freeway back to Melbourne.

Once he was out of sight I drifted towards the giant car park, where there were approximately one thousand identical buses lined up, all of them loading and moving out, heading home to country towns all over Victoria. God knows how long I spent leisurely roaming from one to the other, not a care in the world, trying to spot a familiar Wycheproof face.

It wasn't until night had well and truly fallen and there was only a handful of vehicles remaining in the car park that I concluded I might quite literally have missed the bus. I headed back to the highway, except this time I stood on the northbound side. I didn't attempt to hitch—didn't feel the need. I just stood there, certain the universe would take care of me.

Cars whizzed passed. So did time. I started to doubt the universe.

Gee, what was I going to do? I had to get back to Wycheproof that night, no question, because I had to be at work the next morning. And not just any work: glory be, I had to teach drama to children who were going to grow up to be wheat farmers! I just had to be there, because, well, if I wasn't at school then where the hell would I be?

Still by the side of the Calder, that's where.

'Would you like a lift, Miss Scott?'

It was Barts! Quiet, reserved, handsome Mr Biology Teacher Barts, in his instantly recognisable shiny, bright-green panel van with the gold GT stripe down the side. His housemate, who also taught in Wycheproof, was in the passenger seat. They'd been at the concert.

I climbed aboard and lay down on the mattress in the back. I'd never taken much notice of Barts, but that night, while his housemate dozed, we talked and smoked Winfield Blues and laughed and listened to music the whole way home.

Barts had a girlfriend who lived in Melbourne. He told me about her. I told him about Mr Right.

The following Friday there was a dinner dance at the Wycheproof Shire Hall, with a daggy band playing live music. A few of us schoolteachers went. We all drank and danced. Some of us went back to Barts's place. Eventually, everyone left—except for me. Barts and I sat on the floor in front of the open fire. I happened to mention my fondness for hot water bottles.

'Then how would you like me to be your hot water bottle tonight?'

I told Barts I'd like that very much.

And so Barts and I began a relationship. He bought new red satin sheets for his bed in my honour, and of a night we would lie there smoking Winnie Blues and sharing stories until the early hours. We spent most nights together, because call me crazy but I preferred to be in his bed of red satin than on my own in the farmhouse. In the mornings I had to hide in the back of his panel van, crouched under a blanket, so no-one could see me as he drove me to my house, where I would then get changed and ride my bike to school, a picture of good old-fashioned schoolmarm virtue. Then Barts and I would write poems and letters that we'd leave on one another's desk in the staffroom.

Our love affair was a weekday situation, while on most weekends Barts and I headed off to Melbourne, where we stayed with our respective partners. It's amazing how one can adapt both physically and mentally to such a scenario.

This arrangement continued happily enough until one Monday lunchtime, when Barts asked me to go for a walk. We sat aboard a steam train carriage that had been plonked in the middle of the local park as a 'tourist attraction'. Barts told me he'd ended his relationship with his girlfriend. Toot! Toot! All aboard for a rocky ride!

'Why did you do that, Barts?'

'Because I didn't want to cheat any more.'

Ouch, that hurt. Was it really necessary to use that word—'cheat'?

Barts explained he wanted to be in a legitimate relationship with me, that he loved me.

I was horrified. Not because I didn't love him—I did. But I was also still in love with Mr Right. And, besides, I couldn't be in a relationship with Barts. No way. Even though he was beautiful and kind and loving and fun and we got on like a house on fire and he loved me and I loved him, I could not be in a committed relationship with him because he was too 'ordinary'. He was content to be a high-school teacher and live in the country for the rest of his life. He wanted nothing apart from the love of a good woman and a few kids.

But I was still hanging on to my dream of stardom and the bright lights of Hollywood or, alternatively, the bright lights of Melbourne. The last thing I wanted was to settle down to life on the land, baking sponge cakes for my husband and looking after a dozen kids.

And so, even though I was happier than I'd ever been, living and working in Wycheproof and being with Barts, so driven was I by a compulsion to be extraordinary and live a crazy, non-conservative life that I turned my back on both. I ended my relationship with Barts that day in the park, and at the end of the year I applied for and got a transfer back to Melbourne. My aim: to pursue an acting career and resurrect my relationship with Mr Right.

chapter seven

Upping the ante

By Christmas, my relationship with Mr Right was over. Not that I believed or accepted it: I mean, we were meant to be together forever, right? Of course we'd get back together. It was only a matter of time.

In the meantime I was living back at home with my parents, sleeping in my Queen Anne single bed with the glow-in-the-dark Jesus on the Cross staring down at me. Even though I'd dropped God and Catholicism a few years earlier, I prayed to him and wept profusely, asking for his assistance to please help me and Mr Right get back together.

Christmas Day was the usual—an extended-family do, all of us sitting at trestle tables in the garage—baking—the enforced wearing of bonbon party hats causing me to spiral into a suicidal depression. Was this going to be it? Was I going to be a lonely spinster teacher, living with my parents, for the rest of my life? The thought made me feel sick.

As always happened when I stayed with my parents, I feared that somehow I would be trapped there, never able to get out, that my life would come to a complete standstill. That was how my mother wanted to live, but not me!

Two days after Christmas, like a knight in a shining green panel van, Barts (who had heard of my break-up with Mr Right) arrived at Adeline Street. We'd organised to drive down the Great Ocean Road and have a swim in the sea. When we arrived, we decided to stay a couple of nights. I rang my mother to tell her I wouldn't be coming home. As usual, she asked no questions, but I felt compelled to give her an explanation and so dutifully I lied. I had to. Now that I was living back under her roof, I didn't want to tell her I was staying in the back of a panel van that Barts had reversed onto the top of a cliff so that, as we lay together on the mattress with the doors wide open, we could gaze at the ocean.

What a night!

A few days later Barts rang and asked me to go out with him on New Year's Eve.

I said no.

There were a couple of reasons for this. The first was the possibility I might once more be seduced by Barts's offer of gentle, devoted, stress-free love. What if I ended up staying with him? I needed someone a lot more challenging and difficult, someone whose chemistry, when combined with mine, guaranteed at least some drama, turmoil, and a rollercoaster ride of love and pain that took me from the heights of passion to the depths of fucked-up love gone hideously wrong.

The second reason I couldn't go out with Barts on that New Year's Eve was that I was pretty certain that I would have a great time. All the ingredients were there, and our weekend together at the beach had been exquisitely romantic. But having a good time would really have messed with my head. I felt I hadn't suffered enough over my split with Mr Right, hadn't spent enough uninterrupted time wallowing, hadn't focussed enough on the pain I was feeling.

And so I spent that New Year's Eve at home with my parents in Greensborough, and, trust me, that was suffering.

Staying with my parents over that Christmas break had a profound effect on me. It gave me the courage to get on my bike and ride to Adelaide and not look back. Jane, my teaching buddy from Wycheproof, agreed to come with me.

On the morning of our departure we caught a train to Geelong and commenced our epic journey along the Princes Highway. About ten minutes into our ride we came to a steep descent. I took off at great speed, the wind at my back. Ah, the sense of freedom. Adventure, here we come …

I woke up in Emergency at the Geelong hospital. How was I to know you were meant to pack pannier bags so the weight was spread evenly between them? Poor Jane had been forced to watch in horror as I flew past her, screaming down the hill on a bike that was clearly out of control, its back wheel fishtailing violently. I was nearly at the bottom when the bike flipped, and I did a somersault of sorts, which, according to Jane, was quite spectacular.

My mother and father came to pick me up, and so once more I found myself at my parents' place, this time with my right arm in plaster, my ego bruised and my fear that I would be trapped in Greensborough for the rest of my life gripping me more firmly than ever.

As it turned out, a few weeks later I moved into a share house in North Fitzroy and started teaching drama at Maribyrnong Secondary College.

I hated it.

After the tininess of Wycheproof, Maribyrnong was big and overwhelming. More to the point, after being considered a 'loveable whacko' in Wycheproof, at Maribyrnong I was a big fat nobody, just another teacher flailing about in a huge institution.

I didn't have a boyfriend, and what was I doing about an acting career? Nothing. Absolutely nothing.

I still hadn't learnt that if you want something in life you have to do something to make it happen, not wait for it to come to you. Did I really think that one day Spielberg would just happen to be wandering past my year nine class, that he would peer through the window and see me screaming at a group of fourteen-year-old boys to 'GET INTO A CIRCLE, PLEASE,' slap himself on the forehead and exclaim, 'Oh my God, that's her. She'd be perfect as the love interest in Indiana Jones'? Sadly, yes. That was exactly the way I thought life worked. It was all about timing and luck, nothing to do with making stuff happen yourself.

This philosophy on life wasn't entirely wrong, however; after all, that I finally found the courage to quit teaching and pursue my acting dreams was entirely due to timing and luck. Not that I would call having a head-on car accident exactly *lucky*, but it did change my life for the better. So much better did my life become, in fact, that I've told this story more than a few times before. I'll keep it brief.

I had learnt to drive while I was living in Wycheproof, and I wasn't used to cars coming from the opposite direction. Or perhaps I just wasn't concentrating. Either way, I was travelling along Heidelberg Road when I veered into oncoming traffic.

Miraculously, no-one was hurt. But at the point of impact, what I believed was going to be my last ever thought entered my head: 'Oh Christ, I'm going to die, and I'm going to die a fucking teacher.'

On discovering not only that the other driver was unscathed but also that I was uninjured and, for that day at least, my 'final' thought had been incorrect, I made two resolutions. First, I would never drive again. Second, I would break my contract with the Education Department and quit teaching immediately. It was time to make my own luck.

Hippy house goes to Mindil Beach, Darwin, 1978 — I'm the one with knees
discreetly covering breasts

I'm fourth from the left

chapter eight

Upping the ante a little bit more

As soon as I left my teaching job I found work in the Darwin Theatre in Education team-—the job entailed flying all over the Territory performing shows in schools and Aboriginal settlements and missions. It wasn't Hollywood, but nor was it 'ordinary'.

I moved into a hippie commune: a real, dinky-di hippie commune in Darwin! There were fourteen people living there and two dogs—one called Black Dog and one called Brown Dog, so named because one was black and one was brown. (And yes, being a hippie commune, there were times when the residents got the names of the dogs mixed up.) I was thrilled. How much further off the scale of ordinariness could I possibly get?

There were young children living in the commune with names such as Lily Pond and No-Name—the latter being a four-year-old boy whose mother didn't want to impose a name on him. 'But surely No-Name is as much of a name as Robert or Bill or Edward?' was what I wanted to say to No-Name's mother, but there was no point because she didn't speak, confining herself to primitive grunting noises so as not to impose adult language on her child.

We all slept on mattresses on the floor underneath balsawood pyramids that had been handmade by one of the residents. We fermented our own yoghurt in a large jar that lived on the kitchen bench below its own baby-size pyramid. The entire household was vegetarian, except when we went to barbecues, when everyone seemed to suffer vegetarian amnesia and pigged out on hamburgers.

Given that we were living in a hippie commune in a hot, tropical climate in the late 1970s, everyone walked around in the nude, even me. I still have a group 'family' photo of fifteen of us smiling and naked. I'm sitting cross-legged in the front row in such a way that my knees hide my large non-hippie breasts.

I wrote weekly letters to my parents about my work, the commune, and Aboriginal people. I had never seen an Aboriginal person in my life until I moved to Darwin. You could have knocked me over with a feather the first time I performed in a show for little Aboriginal kids on a mission settlement. While they all laughed and appeared to be enjoying themselves, they seemed insanely reluctant to do anything I asked, such as sing along or wriggle like a snake or clap their hands. What was their problem?

'You're kidding me. They don't speak English?'

Twenty-four years old and I had no idea that the Queen's English was not Aboriginal people's first language.

I told my parents all about it. I figured they didn't have a clue, either. They needed to know this stuff, especially about the issue of racism. I was horrified that segregation existed, that white people treated Aboriginals so poorly, that they lived in such poverty.

My mother always wrote back—it was her job. Dad rarely put pen to paper. Of course, Mum never responded to any of the racism business; no doubt she simply rolled her eyes and shook her head as if to say, 'God, she carries on, doesn't she?' In keeping with being written by a woman of few words, my mother's letters were brief and to the point, one of her most memorable sentences being 'I'm just about to shell some peas for dinner and your grandfather has stomach cancer.' That was it. No more details were given. I was left to sit and wonder: was my mother going to boil the peas, or steam them?

I decided that as part of my 'I'm going to be a no-rules, unconventional sort of gal' mantra I'd give sexual promiscuity a go. The experiment was a total failure.

My first attempt was with a chap who also lived in the commune. On the first and subsequently only night we spent together, lying underneath his pyramid, my hippie neighbour gazed into my eyes and said something no woman ever wants to hear. 'I'm sorry, I don't know why, but I just can't get it up.' It would be an exceptional woman who could hear those words and not immediately conclude that the limp and lifeless appendage in question was without doubt her fault.

Next up (and thankfully this time he *was* up) was a prawn fisherman. I met him at the local pub. He was a beautiful-looking man with whom I had absolutely nothing in common. We had sex on his narrow wooden bunk bed while his sailor mate snored in the bunk above us. It was satisfactory in a 'who cares if it was any good—at least I've done it' kind of way.

However, the next morning, when I went to disembark, I discovered that, while the boat was still technically moored, it had moved during the night and there was now 2 metres of water between me and the dock, and no gangplank in sight. I have never been into sport, especially long jump, but when faced with a crisis the mind can make you do extraordinary things. I took a running leap, my short little legs extending like never before as I flew across the sea, and landed safely on the pier opposite.

Meanwhile, an epic love story was unfolding before our eyes between Sukra and Ravi, aka Leanne and Kevin, who as followers of Guru Rajneesh had both changed their names. They had first met in the commune and had fallen madly in love. All was going well until one day Sukra announced she was leaving Darwin to go and 'find herself' in India.

Ravi was inconsolable. I knew this was the case because while I was at work, busy writing and rehearsing a show called *Mr Long and Mrs Short*, a two-hander named for obvious reasons, I looked up and saw Ravi standing in the doorway, and all he managed to say, or rather splutter, was, 'Oh, Scotty,' whereupon he crumpled to the floor and lay in the foetal position, uncontrollably weeping.

Mr Long tactfully suggested we take a break.

I took Ravi to a nearby park, where we sat together on the grass. I put my arm around his shoulders and listened as he sobbed about how much he loved Sukra and how his heart was breaking and how he didn't think he would ever get over it.

I wanted to say, 'I think you probably will get over it. You were only with her for three weeks,' but instead I told him I was sure they'd be together again soon.

That night I went to the pub with a girlfriend. I decided to wear a black antique French lace dress I'd recently purchased at a hippie market. I met a guy at the bar, we started talking, and I was amazed to find that for the first time since Mr Right I was actually attracted to someone. Like most people in Darwin he was travelling around Australia. When he suggested we go for a walk along Mindil Beach I didn't hesitate. It seemed a little strange that his friend came with us, but at the time I didn't think too much about it.

The three of us were walking along the water's edge when suddenly I found myself flat on my back with the two of them on top of me.

Had I tripped?

I tried to get up.

They wouldn't let me.

I couldn't believe it. Not only had I been really attracted to this guy, but I'd been idiotic enough to believe he was attracted to me and that there had been true chemistry between us, when in fact he and his mate were nothing more than low-life women-hating idiots and, dare I suggest, would-be rapists.

I was furious.

'YOU FUCKING FUCKERS' probably wasn't the best choice of words, given the circumstances, but it seemed to distract them. Or perhaps they weren't really all that committed to their task, because I easily managed to fight them off and make a run for it.

It was late and the commune was quiet when I arrived home. I walked through the lounge, which was dominated by a large wooden dining table. Until recently it had had four legs, but news had arrived from India that sitting on chairs 'messed with your chakra' and overnight the poor table had become a quadruple amputee. Ravi was sitting cross-legged on the floor, his elbows resting on the tabletop, his head in his hands.

He looked up at me, and the moonlight, filtering through the louvre windows, lit up his sad-sack face. 'Oh, Scotty …'

Oh no, for Christ's sake, was he still blubbering about stupid Sukra?

I decided to distract him with my own tale of woe. I sat down on the floor beside him and recounted my evening's adventure.

'Oh, Scotty. That is terrible. It must have been awful. Men can be such bastards.' He took my hand and held it, and we sat in quiet, contemplative silence for some minutes.

Ravi finally broke the silence. 'Scotty …' I turned my face towards his. 'Do you know the best thing we could do right now?'

'What?'

'Fuck.'

Oh my God, was he serious?

Apparently he was, because next thing I knew his open mouth was heading straight towards mine. I pushed him away and told him unequivocally that I wanted neither to pash nor to sleep with him.

'Are you sure, Scotty? It'll do us both good, make us feel so much better.'

Was the guy a complete idiot? Was it not obvious that the last thing I needed after my beach encounter was sex? I needed love!

Later, I lay upon my single foam mattress and considered my promiscuity stats. I counted my list of post–Mr Right lovers. I pondered whether I could include the hippie who couldn't get it up. If not, then that left my tally at one: the prawn fisherman. Not exactly a dazzling result.

There was a quiet knock, and Ravi popped his head around my door. 'Hey, Scotty, just letting you know—if at any time during the night you want to come and get into bed with me, feel free, beautiful girl.'

'Thanks, Ravi, I'll keep it in mind.'

He closed the door and I curled up on my mattress. As exciting as hippie life had been, I decided I needed to move on, do something different.

A few weeks later I quit my job and flew to London.

Actually, I didn't go straight to the motherland. I went via Melbourne. I wanted to see my parents and friends before I left; after all, who knew when I'd be back? If I'd be back?

I had enough money for an airfare to Melbourne, but how boring, safe and mainstream was that? I decided to hitch the 4000 kilometres instead. It must be noted that this was in the good old days, when the name Ivan Milat meant nothing in backpacking circles, and the film *Wolf Creek*, lauded as the most frightening film Australia has ever produced, was still twenty-six years away from being made.

(When *Wolf Creek* premiered in Australia, in 2006, I was doing breakfast radio on a new station called Vega 91.5, which afterwards went on to become known as Classic Rock and is currently Smooth Listening; in other words, it hasn't taken the ratings by storm. As part of my radio-presenting responsibilities I attended a private screening of the film. There was only a handful of people in the theatre, all of us connected to TV or radio programs. I was sitting alone. I found the film terrifying, and all the more so given that the serial killer was John Jarrett, whom I'd only ever known as the loveable larrikin handy-home-hints man on the TV show *Better Homes and Gardens*. During one particularly horrendous scene, in which Jarrett's character is torturing his female victim in the most hideous manner imaginable, I managed to cover my eyes *and* ears so that I could no longer see or hear what was happening. I became aware of a smell. It was a very familiar smell from my childhood days. I lowered my hands and slowly opened my eyes to see fellow comedian and radio presenter Dave O'Neil, who was sitting a few seats away from me, eating a Boston bun and clearly enjoying it, licking the icing from his fingers. He saw me looking at him and offered me a bite. I declined. But forever after I would associate the sweet smell of a Boston bun with torture in the outback.)

But back in 1979, unencumbered by fear of either sticky buns or outback travel, I had no qualms about hitching from Darwin to Melbourne and, it must be said, the trip was awesome. And when I say awesome, I mean awesome in the old-fashioned sense of the word, as in it was overwhelming and wondrous and quite simply the road trip of a lifetime. One of my hippie girlfriends from the commune decided to come with me, and a friend drove us a couple of kilometres out of Darwin and dropped us off at the Stuart Highway. Our first lift took us 300 kilometres, to Katherine. A couple of minutes after we'd been dropped off, an old crimson station wagon pulled up. Three days and 3500 kilometres later, that same vehicle dropped me off at my parents' place in Greensborough.

It was an extraordinary journey: all the kangaroos we saw—admittedly, most of them dead by the roadside—and the wild horses, the donkeys, the cockatoos, even a herd of camels, and a burnt-out, abandoned caravan, and a roadhouse where the man pumping the petrol was as big as King Kong and had a beard to his waist tied into a ponytail with a scrunchy, and all the toasted cheese and tomato sandwiches we ate, and the road trains we passed, and the dust, and the desert, the night sky, the stars, the camp fires, and the fact that I made love to the James Dean–lookalike driver who, okay, may well have been stoned out of his tiny mind, but really was a lovely person—and more to the point doubled my post–Mr Right tally of lovers, taking it to two—all in all, they made it a very memorable trip.

We pulled up outside my parents' house at 9 am. I introduced James Dean to my mother. (My friend from the commune had been dropped off in Adelaide the day before.) He came inside and we had a cup of tea and some toast that Mum made for us. At no point did my mother ask how it came to be that I had arrived home from Darwin in a station wagon with a young man whom it appeared I'd known for only three days.

A week later my parents drove me to the airport. My mother seemed anxious. I later learnt this was because she feared I would never return. It was a valid concern. My aim was to not come home. How would I be able to? With all the adventures I was going to have, not to mention my life taking some crazy, unforseen turn—international fame and fortune and all that—at the very least, I assumed it would be years before I would see my homeland again.

The trip was a disaster. This was entirely my fault: I was stupid, naive and an idiot. How else can I explain why I insisted on hitchhiking on my own? Perhaps it was because my Darwin-to-Melbourne experience had been so positive. I didn't realise that France would be such a different story. Time after time my hitching resulted in men expecting to have sex with me, assuming that was what I also wanted, given I was hitching alone.

Finally, after weeks of nightmarish trips in which I was continuously scared and having to talk my way out of trouble, I decided to stop hitching once and for all. And I did, except for the day I told myself I'd do it just one last time … (*One last time*—oh, the delicious Stephen King overtones; I'm sending a chill up my own spine.)

I was on my way to Saumur, a small village in the south of France. There was a rock concert happening nearby in an ancient castle that I wanted to go to. (Actually, I didn't want to go to it at all—the very thought made me feel lonely and depressed—but I thought I should make the effort, see the country, do something a bit out there.) Since there was no bus or train I had no option but to stand by the side of the road and nonchalantly hold out my index finger.

The trip started off happily enough when a jaunty little bottle-green car pulled up and immediately I felt reassured by the bride and groom dolls sitting on the dashboard. The driver, a young, chubby-faced chap with a friendly smile, explained he'd got married the week before and this had been the wedding car. He told me he was on his way home to his beautiful new wife, and that was why I was so surprised when he undid his fly and suggested I go down on him. And so once more I found myself by the roadside.

I waited and waited and waited.

It was getting late, and I was getting worried, when finally a dusty, mud-covered work vehicle pulled up and I broke a cardinal rule of female hitching: I got into a car with two men. They both had ill-fitting heads and weird teeth and little piggy eyes. Put it this way: they would have been right at home sitting on the front porch playing duelling banjos in the film *Deliverance*.

I sat in the back seat, and they both kept turning around and looking at me. We drove in silence until I saw a sign indicating we were only 3 kilometres from Saumur, and that was when we turned off the main road and began heading down a dirt track into a deep, dark forest of pine trees.

In my halting French I asked what was happening.

The two men looked at one another and grinned and said nothing. I froze, and for the first time in my life I smelt, or rather felt, or maybe it was both smelt and felt, the fear of death.

Once more I asked them what was happening, my overwhelming panic obvious in my cracking, quavering voice.

Once more they looked at each other and grinned, then spoke to one another in rapid French too quick for me to understand. They laughed, and then the chap in the passenger seat turned around and muttered something about having to '*pole fixer d'électricité.*'

Going to fix an electricity pole? In the middle of the bush? I made a deal with God: if I survived this I would never *ever* hitch again.

Eventually we stopped, and both men got out of the car and gestured for me to do the same. I tried to steel myself to do whatever was needed in order to survive. I told myself that even though I was about to endure being raped, if I kept my wits about me they might let me live. The thought of staying alive no matter what had an extremely strong appeal at that point in time.

The two piggy-eyed inbreds just stood there, eerily silent, staring at me. There was no point running anyway: there was nowhere to run. Nor was there any point calling for help: there was no-one to hear. And so I too stood there, paralysed with fear and the knowledge that there was not a single soul in the entire world, apart from these two men, who knew where I was.

They moved towards me, and my resolve to stay calm disappeared. I started to scream. It was involuntary. I couldn't stop. I screamed my lungs out. The men said something but I wasn't listening; the closer they came, the louder I screamed. Closer and closer they moved towards me, and then, to my astonishment, they passed me and went to the back of the car. They opened the boot and pulled out a tool box, and blow me down if they didn't then walk towards an electricity pole. Who'd have thought?

Five minutes later they returned to the car. I had no choice but to get in. We headed back down the track to the main road, and ten minutes later they dropped me off at Saumur.

I got out of the car.

None of us spoke.

Was it a simple misunderstanding, or did those men want to torment me or, worse, intend to do me harm and for some reason changed their minds? *Je ne sais pas.* All I knew was I was alive and therefore had to keep my promise to God to never hitch again.

Except I had to hitch again, because the castle was in Fontevraud, a further 15 kilometres out of Saumur.

I could not believe my eyes when a car pulled over and there in the driver's seat was a drop-dead gorgeous, young and friendly Frenchman who was also on his way to the festival. His name was Randolph, and *mon dieu*! What with his long dark hair pulled back in a ponytail, high cheekbones and flaw-less skin, I couldn't help but imagine us making love in front of a log fire. Oh dear, if only I hadn't eaten all those butter croissants and if only I didn't have a pimple the size of a walnut on my chin and if only I wasn't wearing stiff new half-mast army pants, thick red explorer socks and tan walking boots, and if only I'd washed my greasy hair, and come to think of it if only I'd had a shower in the previous week, and if only I'd worn some make-up and, oh, if only I wasn't giving off such a lonely, pathetic, miserable vibe, maybe I would have been in with a chance. Oh Randolph, if only …

From the outside, the castle was your classic medieval situation: grand and glorious, evoking images of trumpeters heralding the arrival of gallant knights on horseback while they are greeted by young, fair-skinned maidens in brocade velvet gowns. Inside was quite a different story. The place was packed with drunks, some of them vomiting. It made me homesick for Australia.

At the end of the concert I made my way up the nearby hill to a makeshift camping ground, where I attempted to erect my one-man tent. I'd done it many times before, but that night I just stood there staring down at the canvas and the poles and the pegs wondering how on earth they all pieced together. I think my vagueness had something to do with the joint I'd smoked earlier at the castle. A chap had handed it to me, and while normally I would have refused I was so lonely and longing to hear Billy Thorpe singing 'Rock me baby' instead of the French shit I was being forced to endure that I had thrown caution to the wind. I hadn't intended to smoke the whole thing, but when I went to hand it back my new friend was nowhere to be seen and I didn't know what else to do, and so, before I knew it, it was all gone. And so, may I say, was I.

A group of French revellers offered to help me with my tent, but it quickly became apparent that they were in pretty much the same mental state as me, and all we managed to do was laugh. So eventually it was suggested I stay in one of their tents. Gratefully I accepted and crawled into a three-man tent, where I squeezed in beside two men and another woman. The four of us lay there like sardines, but within minutes the chap next to me went the grope, which didn't surprise me; after all, I had bad body odour and was still wearing my jumper, army pants and thick socks. Why wouldn't he be sexually aroused?

Wearily, I sat up and prepared to head off to God knew where, but to my surprise this young chap apologised and told me to stay put, because since I clearly wasn't interested in sex he was happy to leave and see if he could get some action in another tent. So I stayed where I was and soon fell asleep.

It didn't last long. I woke to find the couple next to me in the throes of an extraordinarily vigorous lovemaking session. I tried my best to stay out of their way, but given the tininess of the tent and the acrobatic nature of their tryst it wasn't easy. They were licking and slapping and kissing and spinning around and sitting on top of one another; at one point he went up into a sort of handstand, as much as the tent allowed, and landed with his penis in the girl's face, which was just as well because for one ghastly second I thought it was going to land in mine. Then he began to make a noise not too dissimilar to a donkey's—the point being it was loud.

And then suddenly there was a blinding flash of light inside the tent.

I sat up in fright. So did the lovemaking couple.

It turned out that the couple's friends who were camped nearby had decided to sneak up, throw open the fly of the tent and take a surprise flash photo of the event. So some-where, stuck on a fridge in southern France, I like to think, there exists a photo of a naked French couple and a fully dressed Australian woman sitting bolt upright, looking straight down the barrel of the camera, mouths and eyes wide open in shock.

I suffered dreadful homesickness, and so, less than three months after leaving Australia, I returned home, tail between my legs, feeling lost, depressed and fat. In case I was in any doubt about the last of these, the first thing my mother said upon seeing me at the airport was, 'Good God, Denise, is that *all* you?'

It wasn't just homesickness that brought me back to Australia; I was also lovesick. Or maybe it was just loneliness. Either way, the whole time I was in Darwin and Europe—and, trust me, this is a painful admission—I had continued to write letters to Mr Right: upbeat, cheery tomes that sometimes included a funny drawing or a photo or a poem I'd written, all designed to make him aware of what a truly amazing individual I was—brilliant, unique …

He never wrote back.

Now, most people of sound mind, given their ex did not respond in any way, would have concluded that their ex was happy to be just that—an ex. But I wasn't of sound mind. And so, as soon as I arrived home from Europe, I called him and said I needed to see him. Could he come over?

He said he couldn't.

I said please.

He said no, he couldn't, because he didn't have enough petrol in his car.

I suggested he go to a service station and fill it up.

He said he didn't have any money.

(But how could this be? He had a full-time job and was a cautious spender.)

I said I would pay for him to put petrol in his car.

He muttered something about being too busy.

I kind of begged then, explaining that I needed to ask him something.

He suggested I ask him over the phone.

I said that I had to do it face to face.

And so finally he agreed.

He arrived. I greeted him at the front door, and we went and sat in the backyard underneath the oleander—a tree noteworthy for its poisonous sap.

Without so much as an informal warm-up chat about the weather, I asked, 'Do you think you could ever love me again?'

Without a second's hesitation he said, 'No. I've met someone else and I'm in love with them.'

Oh well, rightio then. As you were, everyone.

'Denise, what are you doing?'

My mother had followed me down the garden path, cigarette in hand. I was dragging two green garbage bags behind me that I had just retrieved from my parents' garage, where I had my few possessions in storage. I was heading to the grey-brick incinerator located at the far end of the yard. When I arrived at my destination, my mother came and stood next to me. She asked again what I was doing.

I told her I was going to burn my diaries, two full bags of them. I had written daily entries in them since I was twelve.

'Are you sure you want to do that?'

'Yes, I'm positive.'

'Why?'

I'd read in one of my New Age hippie books that it was a way of cleansing one's soul, a way of letting go of the past. But I didn't bother telling my mother this, assuming it would make no sense to her.

'Denise, why don't you wait and have a think about it?'

'Because I don't want to, Mum. I just want to burn them.'

'Please, Denise, please wait.' It was weird that my mother was speaking to me like this. She was the greatest getter-ridder of stuff I knew. 'Denise, what about in years to come? Maybe you'll want to read them.'

'I won't, Mum.'

'Well, you might want to use them, turn them into a book or something.'

(How right she was. If only I'd listened to her this whole writing thing would've been so much easier.)

'Mum, I don't want to read what's in these diaries and I certainly wouldn't want anyone else to.'

'Oh Denise, please wait …'

Too late.

I lit the match and up they went.

Thoughts, hopes, dreams, doubts, triumphs, arguments, embarrassments; Spirax notebooks full of words and pictures, hardback diaries with gold-lined pages, a 1971 desktop calendar, a pink diary with a key, exercise books: all disappeared before my eyes. Their demise was quick. My father, not usually associated with handyman status, had constructed an extraordinarily efficient incinerator, the air being sucked in from underneath, making the flames whoosh. Within minutes there was nothing but a small pile of ash.

I walked back towards the house, passing my mother, who stood there staring at the incinerator, looking strangely distraught.

Hitching in Scotland, 1979

chapter nine

Passing the baton

There is no doubt in my mind that oppression—
that burdensome weighing down of the mind by
past hurts and shame—gets passed from one generation to
another. I know this for a fact; Dr Phil told me. And what a
powerful beast it is, oppression: almost impossible to fight or
shake off, much easier to just accept and live your life accordingly, never asking questions, never arguing, never saying what
you really think, never taking a risk: better to keep your head
down, your mouth shut, and stay away from trouble. That was
what I learnt from my mother. I hasten to add that I also learnt
brilliant things from my mother—the importance of family,
love, kindness; taking joy in the simple things in life: sharing a
meal or a cuppa, doing some gardening, going for a walk and
taking the time to look up and admire the beauty of the sky.
But I became aware that there was an oppressive force with a
hold over my family soon after returning from my ill-fated
overseas trip. I was staying with my parents. At twenty-four
years of age I didn't have a job, didn't have a boyfriend and
didn't have anywhere else to live—it wasn't a high point.

It was a summer evening and we had just finished dinner, and my mother and I were lying on newly purchased yellow plastic banana lounges in the backyard. My father was inside doing the dishes, a task he had willingly embraced after my sister and I left home.

As usual, my mother lit up an Albany cigarette. Out of the corner of my eye I watched her slowly and lovingly inhale and exhale. I longed for one, but I still hadn't found the courage to admit to her I smoked. My sister hadn't admitted to it, either. Given that Mum was a thirty-a-day woman, it may appear odd that we couldn't confess our nicotine habit to her, but the reason was simple: she would have disapproved.

My mother, as was her wont, commented on the evening sky. 'Look at that sunset. Isn't it beautiful? Looks as though it's going to be warm tomorrow.' There was a slight pause before she continued. 'Denise, there's something I want to tell you.'

Oh God, don't tell me I'm adopted. Surely not! My eyeballs—they're identical to my father's.

'May wasn't my sister. She was my mother.'

Wow! I was not expecting that.

Once that bombshell had been dropped, it seemed to spark an avalanche of information. Mum told me May had been fifteen years old when, in 1924, she had given birth to my mother, Marg, 'father unknown'. Such was the family's shame, typical of the era, that it was decided my mother would be raised by May's parents, Ma and Pa Bock, as May's baby sister. Two years later, at seventeen years of age, May became pregnant again and gave birth to a second daughter. This time May married the father, and they moved to Tatura.

Family rumour had it that the shock of May's second pregnancy caused her mother, Ma Bock, to die at a relatively young age. Her death meant that my mother was now without a mother, because her real mother (May) had gone to live elsewhere and her pretend mother (Ma Bock) was no longer alive.

At this point I was forced to interrupt. 'So, hang on, Mum, this means Pa Bock wasn't my grandfather; he was …'

'Your great-grandfather. Is that right?'

Even Mum was confused.

She lit another cigarette. As I desperately attempted to breathe in her second-hand smoke, she continued, 'Yes, that must be right, because Pa Bock was May's father, so that means he was my grandfather, so your great-grandfather.'

It seemed Mum was on a roll. There was no stopping her. She retold me her family's story, but this time, unlike that time at the kitchen sink when I asked who Pa Bock was, she didn't head me off at the pass: she told me the truth. Pa Bock had indeed remarried after Ma Bock, May's mother, died, and Bridie, an Irishwoman, had come to the marriage with a half-dozen or so children.

This meant my four-year-old mother had been living with her grandfather (who she believed was her father), her step-grandmother (who she believed was her stepmother) and a tribe of Irish step-uncles and step-aunts (who she believed were her step-siblings), the youngest one being Peggy, she of the 'day the custard caught' fame. When I was sixteen my mother had said that Bridie hadn't been very nice to her. In fact, Bridie had loathed my mother and was mean to her. She had tormented her cruelly, making her sit on a stool in the hallway next to where the old-fashioned wind-up phone hung on the wall. Bridie would pretend to call the police and ask them to come and take my mother away and put her in jail for being a naughty girl.

On one occasion my mother was so terrified of going to jail that she ran away. The police were called for real, and the whole town gathered to join in the search for the missing child. The fact that my mother had only got as far as hiding under the house increased her fear. Crouched in a tiny ball, hidden from view, she watched the feet of all the locals coming and going. Too frightened to come out, aware of the trouble she would be in, she stayed hidden for hours. When she finally emerged, a local chap grabbed her and held her aloft. 'She's been found!' Everyone cheered, thrilled that the child was safe. No-one cared about the fact that she had just been hiding under the house. Except Bridie. She was not happy, not happy at all.

And so at five years of age my mother was sent to live with a foster family. The foster family abused her.

Mum didn't give me many details of the abuse, except that the boys in the foster family forced her to drink their urine out of a little cup, part of a tea set my mother cherished. After she had been with the family for some months, one of her Irish 'stepbrothers' arrived in a horse and cart to visit her. He was horrified by the situation he found her in and took her back to live once more with Pa Bock and Bridie.

But Bridie's detestation of Mum had continued unabated, and my mother was sent to live with her 'sister', May, and her husband, and their ever-expanding brood of children. Mum loved her 'big sister' and adored her 'nieces' and 'nephews' (who were actually her half-siblings), especially the eldest, Noreen.

When my mother was fifteen, she was walking home from the local hotel where she worked as a cleaner. (She left school at fourteen.) As she passed a large vacant block a couple of local boys called out to her. She was familiar with them and so stopped to chat.

They tried to rape her.

A local man came riding past on his pushbike, and Mum managed to call out to him. He didn't hear her, but it was enough of a distraction, and my mother made a run for it. She got away from the boys and arrived home hoping to sneak into the house and tell no-one of her ordeal. But as she came around the corner of the house she ran smack-bang into May. My mother's dress was ripped and covered in dirt. She was crying.

May forced her to say what had happened. My mother begged her not to do anything, but there is nothing on earth as ferocious as a mother's protective instincts when her child has been hurt, even if the mother–daughter bond has never been acknowledged. May went to the police to get justice for her 'younger sister' and to make sure her attackers were punished. The two boys were charged with attempted rape. A court case was held in Bendigo. Mum didn't tell me what the outcome was, but she did tell me that afterwards her life became hellish.

The two boys had been from the 'good side' of town, from well-to-do families who looked down upon people like my mother. After the court case Mum was ostracised by many of the locals for getting those poor boys into trouble. Who did that little tramp think she was? One day, one of the boy's mothers passed Mum in the street and spat on her and called her a bastard. My mother told me that throughout her life to that point she had often been called a bastard but hadn't known why.

It was around this time that May's sister-in-law, who cared a great deal for my mother, suggested she look for her birth certificate. She found it in a cupboard and learnt for the first time that May was her mother, not her sister.

My mother said nothing about it to anyone.

When she was twenty-two, living in Melbourne and about to marry my father, my mother was told that if she could produce a parent's signature for some particular bit of paperwork it would make the marriage process a lot more straightforward. And so she wrote to May, telling her she knew she was her mother and that all she wanted was for May to sign the document; she promised never to mention their secret again. May never signed the document or acknowledged the letter. She and her husband went to my parents' wedding, famously bringing a freshly decapitated and plucked chook wrapped in newspaper as a gift for my father's family.

My mother had one final shock for me that evening. 'Now, Denise, your dad knows about this but no-one else. So please promise me you won't tell anyone. Not even your sister.'

Was she for real? Not tell my sister? Julie and I never kept secrets. We told one another everything. How could I possibly keep something like this from her? Apart from anything else it didn't seem fair for me to know something so important about our family and my sister not. But Mum was adamant. She was worried Julie would tell her husband. 'And what if he has a few drinks and says something at a family do?'

I deeply regretted not being able to share these revelations with my sister. They helped explain so many things about Mum. Why she so yearned for the ordinary: not because she had come from an ordinary family, but quite the opposite, and now what she craved was a straightforward, uncomplicated family life. Why she loved my dad's family so much: because they had welcomed her with open arms, invited her into their home and loved her unashamedly. Why she so loved my dad's father: because she'd never had one. Why she'd been so stricken with grief at May's funeral: because not only had she lost her mother but she had lost the possibility of ever having her mother acknowledge her as her daughter. And, of course, that was why Pa Bock had been so cold and distant when we visited and why everyone had been so surprised to see him at May's funeral: because he was ashamed of her and my mother and what they represented. I recalled telling my mother about a friend who'd had a tough time growing up because her parents had gone through a messy divorce, and how Mum had scoffed, 'What would she know about tough times? She's had it easy.' At the time I had been taken aback by her dismissive tone—it had seemed inappropriately harsh—but now I understood where she had been coming from.

Why did my mother reveal her secret to me on that particular evening? Was it something to do with me burning my diaries? At the time she had been so horrified, standing at the incinerator, watching all those memories going up in flames, disappearing without a trace. She had appeared so desperate for that not to happen. Did she fear the same fate for her own memories, especially her secrets, those secrets that she'd carried for so long, all on her own, at least until she met my father? Did she fear that they'd disappear without trace? Did she determine there and then that there was no way that was going to happen, that she had to make sure there was at least one other person besides Russ who knew exactly what she had been through in her life?

Whatever her reasons, one thing was clear. Just like my mother and father before me, I was now, albeit very reluctantly, a keeper of the family secret.

Well hello!! Suddenly life was well and truly extraordinary and yet there I was, absolutely desperate for it to be ordinary again. I snuck out the front door and walked around the corner to Beewar Street. Until that night it had never occurred to me how close the name was to 'beware', such ominous overtones: 'Beware the extraordinary, it ain't always pretty.' I looked around; the coast was clear, there was no-one in sight. Thank God for that! I went and hid behind a tree and smoked a cigarette.

chapter ten

The call of the wild

At twenty-five years of age I was still single, living on my own in a small flat in St Kilda, doing a bit of acting and a lot of waitressing, and forever feeling on the brink of overwhelming panic that I'd never find love again.

And then I met John.

It was meant to be. Really it was—of that I have no doubt. It was towards the end of 1980 and I'd applied for a full-time job with Popular Theatre Troupe, a left-leaning community theatre company based in Brisbane. A performer named John Lane had recently left the group, meaning there was a spot up for grabs. I flew to Brisbane, auditioned, and got the gig.

In the meantime, the aforementioned John Lane decided to take a year off to travel around Australia, departing from his hometown, Melbourne. First stop: Albury, 314 kilometres north on the Hume Highway. He intended to stay for one night before moving on but that evening he met up with a friend of a friend of a friend, Mark Shirrefs, who just happened to be one of the directors of the Murray River Performing Group, a local professional theatre company. As usual, John had his ukulele, juggling balls and kazoo with him, and no doubt he spontaneously performed a casual backflip while walking down the street. He was that sort of guy. Mark was impressed and immediately offered John a job with the MRPG's brand-new clown ensemble. John accepted, and thus his year long 'hitching around Australia' adventure came to an abrupt stop only a few hours out of Melbourne.

At the same time, only a few days before I had to fly to Brisbane to start my new job, a friend rang. 'Hey Scotty, have you heard, the MRPG are setting up a clown ensemble and I know for a fact they're still looking for one more clown—it's got to be a woman. Why don't you audition?'

Why? Because I'd already accepted the job in Brisbane. And, oh yes, that's right—I hated clowning, couldn't stand it, had no interest. Then again, Albury was a lot closer to Melbourne than Brisbane, and I did have some friends already living there, and I'd heard on the grapevine that this new clown troupe was aiming to be experimental and create clowns for adults, ooh la la, so …

I got the job. God knows why because for my audition, since I couldn't juggle or cartwheel, I decided to go for pathos instead and I earnestly sang an a cappella version of the Beatles hit song 'Help'.

I rang Brisbane and apologised, explaining I would no longer be coming.

And so it was that on 11 January 1981, John (who was meant to be on the road) and I (who was meant to be taking over the job he'd recently vacated in Brisbane) both reported for duty at clown headquarters in downtown Albury. The five clowns had a meeting together and then for some reason, I like to think it was fate, John and I ate lunch together. It was just the two of us, sitting on the ground in a small park in the main street, eating takeaway vegetarian pies, John thinking, God she's got great breasts, and me thinking, God he's got a beautiful body, so fit and muscular. And I love his cheek bones and the way his shirt is missing all the buttons—his torso is fucking gorgeous, and what a smile. He seems so happy and positive and oh my God, I don't believe it, he's juggling an apple and an orange and his empty drink bottle. What a talented guy. Wonder if I should I confess to him that I can't juggle, in fact have an extreme fear of balls? No, why bother, that'll become obvious soon enough. Oh good Lord, he's doing stretches, what a show-off. But God, he really has got a great body, look at his calf muscles, and he's so flexible, wonder if he does yoga? I love that cool stud he's got in his ear, wonder what it is, oh wow, it's a blowfly, a sterling silver blowfly! That is so cool …

And call it cute or call it absolutely sickening, but the clown characters we developed, Puff (me) and Drippins (John), quickly developed a strong flirtatious attraction for one another that knew no bounds—the day John, or rather Drippins, was arrested being a case in point. We were participating in a street parade in the New South Wales town of Orange when John/Drippins was taken into custody by the local police for skating through a red light. He wasn't skating (how could he have been, there was no ice in Orange), he was miming skating—that's how good at clowning he was! I, or rather Puff, marched into that police station, a clown/woman with a large round ball of a body, a bathing cap on my head and full clown make-up on my face, and refused to leave until I'd got justice for my man Drippins, who was duly let off with a warning to not skate through a red light ever again.

Less than four weeks after our first meeting John and I were not only in a committed relationship, but had declared—not that we were in any hurry—that we wanted to have kids together.

Two clowning years later, in 1983, we returned to Melbourne and moved in to a house together.

Then, on 27 August of that same year, Mum rang me with the news. 'Denise, it's your dad. He's not too good.' That was my mother's way of saying Dad had died.

He was at home in bed when the heart attack happened. My mother had always been fanatical about ambulance cover—it was the one thing she regularly pestered me about. 'Have you got ambulance cover, Denise? You never know when you'll need it.' And yet that morning she didn't call an ambulance. Was she in denial over how serious the situation was? Or did Dad insist she not make a fuss? Whatever her reasoning, Mum didn't call an ambulance, and Dad died in the back seat of a taxi on the way to hospital. Mum never, and I mean never, forgave herself.

The morning after Dad died there was a gathering of family members, including some of Dad's siblings, my 'cousin' Noreen, my sister, Julie, and, of course, John. We were all seated around the kitchen table while Mum cooked up a storm—bacon, eggs and toast—keeping moving, keeping busy, keeping from facing her unbearable loss.

Noreen was composing her death notice for Dad for the newspaper. She looked up and asked, 'Who should I say it's from? Russ's loving niece?'

'Oh, for God's sake, Noreen, you're not my niece. You're my sister.'

For a split second, time stood still, like a freeze frame, as everyone in the kitchen paused in what they were doing to absorb the words my mother had just uttered. And then life resumed once more. Bacon and eggs were served up, Noreen signed off on her notice as my father's 'loving sister-in-law' and Uncle Ken poured us all a brandy.

A few months after my father's death, I became pregnant with our first child. I went to my mother's house to deliver the news and burst into uncontrollable sobs. I thought she would be unhappy because John and I weren't married. But Mum could sometimes surprise me. When I announced John and I were going to get married (purely to please her), she responded, 'Oh, Denise, do you really think you should do that? You and John seem to have such a great relationship. It'd be a pity to go and spoil it.'

And so John and I remained true to our Goldie Hawn–Kurt Russell status. We bought the house we still live in, Number 26, in a location near my mother's house. We visited her at least once a week, I rang her most days, and John was always on call to drop everything and race out to change a light globe, replace the fire alarms, move furniture, drive her to appointments and bring her to our place to share meals and celebrate grandkids' birthdays and other family events.

But as much as we tried to lift her spirits and she tried to get back on her feet, my mother never recovered from my father's death. The light in her life had gone out.

Six years after my father died I became a stand-up comedian.

I was thirty-four years old when I received the call, not from God but from his opposite—not that I'm saying comedy is of the devil, but it is irreverent, rude and profane; at least, that's my experience of it. I like to refer to it as the 'call of the wild', because stand-up comedy for me was a wild choice. It positively stank of the extraordinary, reeked of adventure, dripped with risk-taking edginess. And, God knows, at that stage of my life I needed to recharge my 'extraordinary' status.

Because at thirty-four I was ordinary. (Is there really such a thing? Even the Greek woman who lives across the road from me—who, whenever I ask how she is, replies, 'Oh, you know, every day the same'—has an interesting limp.) By 'ordinary' I mean that apart from the odd performing job I was a full-time stay-at-home mum with two children, who were four and five years old. I hadn't intended to stop working, but to my surprise I found I couldn't leave my kids—just couldn't bring myself to do it, couldn't bear to be apart from them. At least, that's my story and I'm sticking to it. (Truth be told, it wasn't only because I couldn't stand to be separated from my children; it was also because I didn't have a lot of options. Hollywood wasn't exactly calling. No-one was calling. And, just quietly, I was relieved.)

I was over trying to be extraordinary. It was exhausting and relentless, not to mention stressful. The constant sense of failure, never achieving my goal of feeling amazing, certainly never reaching the dizzying heights of glory I had experienced when I won Miss Junior Watsonia, left me feeling, for want of a more literary description, absolutely shithouse. In contrast, those carefree 'ordinary' days of hanging out with my kids were blissful—making play dough, going to the park, mooching at home. Godammit, I loved being ordinary! Living in an ordinary house in an ordinary suburb, doing ordinary things, being an ordinary mum: it was as though I'd been let out of prison, freed from the burden of striving to be extraordinary. Of course, there were, as my mother had found, obstacles to ordinariness: John, for instance—his street-performing work as a clown, which often meant him leaving home dressed in drag as a policewoman and armed with a meat cleaver and an apple to juggle—was not ordinary.

But at thirty-four I became restless. The play dough was no longer enough, and, besides, the 'extraordinary' was once again calling me, seducing me with its evil charm. I couldn't resist. I had friends who had started doing stand-up, and I thought, Why not? I came from a funny family, didn't I? And had I not made the other parents laugh themselves sick when I hosted a Trivial Pursuit night at the kids' kindergarten fundraiser? Clearly, I was meant, born, to be a stand-up! More than likely I'd have my own TV show within a year—in the States! And it was the sort of job that meant I could look after my kids and have a career at the same time. How brilliant!

How naive! It was hell!

Nevertheless, with the help (and sometimes hindrance) of John, we made it work in our own crazy, chaotic, stressful way.

What really made my life as a comedian hell, though, had nothing to do with juggling it with motherhood. Just being a comedian made me feel sick, really sick—sick to the pit of my stomach.

When I first decided to become a stand-up I assumed I was going to be brilliant at it. Truly, I had no doubt I was going to be the next Lucille Ball, or, to bring it closer to home, I was going to fill the rather large shoes of Australia's King of Comedy, Graham Kennedy. God knows, I may not have had his male genitalia but I sure as hell had his eyeballs. But then, knock me down with a feather, it turned out I wasn't brilliant at all. Sure, I may have jumped to that conclusion a little pre-maturely—after one gig—but nevertheless my failure to take the world by storm was a terrible kick to the guts. I couldn't believe it. Me! Denise Scott! Miss Junior Watsonia 1964! Not brilliant as a comedian?

There is a theory that my lack of immediate success was due to the stink of fear—the audience could smell my terror as soon as I walked onstage. I'm sure it was more complex; whatever the reason, the fact was that my career didn't take off. As a means of survival I gradually lowered my comedy expectations until I aimed to do nothing more than be a good stand-up—by no means the best, just good. I determined that I would not quit until I had achieved that goal. If anyone had told me it would take twenty years, I no doubt would have said, 'Fuck that for a joke' and given up there and then. But no-one did tell me …

And so for the next twenty years I pursued a career that made me feel ill. Not all the time: I had some great experiences along the way, doing shows with Judith Lucy and the late Lynda Gibson, and the Comedy Festival show I wrote and performed with my nineteen-year-old son. But more often than not I found the job torturous—not so much the twenty minutes I spent onstage, but the lead-up and aftermath, especially the aftermath. Rarely did I come offstage feeling good about myself. Often I'd go home, get into bed, hide under my doona, curl up in the foetal position and palpably burn with a deep sense of shame. I'd lie there groaning (and no, I wasn't pissed, although I admit I behaved in exactly the same manner after a big night out). Groaning and hiding, I would relive the stupid things I'd said or done onstage.

Sometimes this shame was entirely warranted. There was the time I hosted the Jenny Craig awards night for all their centre managers and when one of them walked across the stage to accept her award I noticed she only had one arm, because I'm quite observant like that, and I said, 'I realise the pressure's on to lose weight, but …' I didn't get asked to do that gig the following year.

Then there was the Our Lady of Mercy College centenary dinner, but I blame the organising committee for that debacle: they were the ones stupid enough to invite me to be their *only* speaker. All I did was say 'Yes.' I was genuinely thrilled to be asked. I had loved my time there and assumed, very wrongly, as it turned out, that it would be a hoot—a love fest of crazy, fun-loving Catholic-school girls reliving those wild days of youth.

I admit, I was surprised when I rocked up for the dinner and discovered everyone was really quite conservative. Some were wearing crucifixes on chains around their necks! Were they nuns? I wasn't sure. They could easily have been—they were also wearing extremely comfortable shoes. But then again so was I. And gee, some of those women were old! They looked ancient; I almost felt a need to dust off the cobwebs, that was how old they looked, which quite frankly made a nice change, as usually when I performed comedy *I* was the geriatric in the room. After a few subtle enquires I managed to confirm that there were indeed a few nuns present, including an adored ex-principal who was being treated with such reverence that I suspected that had her former pupils followed their gut instincts they would have thrown themselves on the floor and lain prostrate at her feet.

Given the conservative vibe of the room I decided to forgo my opening line, which was 'Our Lady's was your typical Catholic girls school—you know, full of loose, easy sluts,' although it seemed such a shame to lose it: it always went down a treat in the stand-up venues. As I waited to go onstage a mantra was going around inside my head: 'Don't say fuck. Don't say fuck. Don't say fuck. Don't say fuck.' This was weird, because I rarely did use that word onstage, especially at formal events.

So why did I say it that night?

Actually, it wasn't the first thing I said, which was, 'So, how many of us here have lapsed?' From the deafening silence, I gathered I was the only one.

And then I said it. *That* word. Why did I do that? It was because I was talking about our old sports uniforms and how they were white cotton frocks with knee-length pleated skirts and what a fucking-fucker they were to iron. Because they *were* a fucking-fucker to iron. But I didn't say 'fucking-fucker'; I just said 'fucker', so I did make a compromise for the nuns.

The silence in the room at that point of the proceedings was very deep.

The next words to come out of my mouth were accompanied by the distinct clicking sound that started when, aware of the phenomenal debacle I was in the midst of, my mouth stopped producing saliva and consequently I began to open and close it, clicking my tongue and trying to swallow in a desperate bid to create some moisture. I was spiralling out of control, nosediving towards disaster. I had to pull a rabbit out of the hat. Sadly, I pulled the wrong rabbit. I began to rave mindlessly about the fact that our sports dresses were white. 'White dresses! Adolescent girls! White dresses! White! Adolescent girls! White dresses! Do I have to explain myself?' Tragically, that night, I did. I told the story of how in 1970 I'd seen 'Joanna Murphy run to first base on the softball field with a blood stain on the back of her dress the size and shape of Europe—including Italy in the shape of a boot.'

Gee, I hadn't thought the silence could go any deeper, but blow me down it did.

Now I was having an out-of-body experience, possibly a panic attack. I was looking down at myself onstage, screaming, 'SHUT UP! SHUT UP! SHUT UP!' But I couldn't shut up. I couldn't stop the words coming out of my mouth. Now I was raving on about the burners. For those unfamiliar with burners, back in our day we didn't have nice pale-grey Rentokil bins with pale-pink lids that men in overalls and gloves and masks came to collect every other day; no, we had mini incinerators attached to the wall of each toilet cubicle. 'I'm telling you, on a hot day, if they were downwind, girls just fainted. We had to step over their bodies …' A hundred years of school history, and I chose to talk about the burners.

What a nightmare for the poor organiser of that dinner, such a lovely woman. I burnt with shame for months afterwards.

A couple of weeks after the centenary debacle I ran into an old friend, who introduced me to her nineteen-year-old daughter, who was studying to become a psychologist. I told them about the dinner and how I hadn't seemed to be able to control what I was saying. The young up-and-coming psychologist became excited. 'We've just been studying that sort of thing at college, and apparently what happens is when people get older their brain pushes onto the frontal lobe, which is where all your inhibition factors are, and loosens them up, and that's why old people start swearing and saying what they think, so that's probably what's happening to you.'

Well, thank you, Little Miss Gen Y. Such comforting news.

My mother hated my comedy. I realise 'hate' is a strong word, but on one of the rare occasions when she said what she thought after seeing me do a routine on TV, 'hate' was the exact word she used.

The rational part of me accepted this situation. How could I possibly expect my mother, a woman born in 1924, raised in an extremely conservative Catholic family in a small country town, to approve of my work? She didn't think stand-up was a suitable profession for a lady. As I've mentioned, she hated swearing, especially when the expletives were uttered by women or, more specifically, by her daughter, or, even more specifically, by her daughter when standing alone at a microphone onstage. She also thought poorly of people telling personal stories to friends, yet alone telling them to Bert Newton on national TV. And as for failing in public, something she thought I managed to do with unbelievable aplomb: the concept was unbearable for her.

I told myself that parental approval was not a right. You couldn't expect a human being to love and encourage what you did just because they'd given birth to you. Just ask Mrs Hitler or Mrs Pol Pot. Not that I'm suggesting that having a child who became a stand-up comic is the same as having a child who became a mass murderer, although I suspect that had I become the latter my mother's reaction would have been much the same—a grim, stoic, silent acceptance of a disappointing and shameful situation. But deep down my mother's disapproval of my work hurt and often made me angry. I know, I know: if I was reading this I'd be thinking the same thing. Oh, poor Denise. Boo hoo! What a hard life. Fancy having a mother who didn't praise you for saying 'fuck' and telling stories about smoking vaginas onstage. No wonder she's written a book about it. Such cruelty! It makes *Angela's Ashes* read like a picnic.

The only time my mother ever saw me perform in my own show was in 2000. I had written *Suburban Riot*, and it was being shown as part of the Melbourne International Comedy Festival. Mum had heard that during the show I talked about her and the time the fires had come close to Greensborough, so she and her sister Noreen came to check it out.

I was performing in the Melbourne Town Hall. For those picturing the main hall, which seats fifteen hundred people, let me clarify: I was in the 'cloakroom', a small room that seats about a hundred.

I will never forget how sick I felt that night standing backstage and looking through the slight crack between the double wooden doors and seeing my mother and aunt marching down the grand marble hallway towards the venue. How my stomach heaved, and how I prayed with all my heart that the earth would open up and swallow me, or at the very least bring on a mild stroke that meant I couldn't perform—anything rather than have my mother in the audience. Of course, there was a contradiction going on here. On the one hand, all I wanted was my mother to acknowledge my work; on the other, when she did show up I literally wanted to die.

As showtime drew near I went over my script in my head and groaned, knowing for sure and certain my mother would hate it, especially my Rage Against the Machine routine, and specifically my observations regarding their song 'Killing in the name'. For those unfamiliar with the song, the lyrics include several appearances of the f-word. In my routine I proposed that this song was all well and good but asked what the young fans would do in their old age for their weekly singalong in the retirement village, whereupon I proceeded to sing the 'no way, get fucked, fuck off' lyrics as an elderly woman might, with a sweet, quavering, church choir voice. I guess you had to be there … which, unfortunately, my mother was.

I was halfway through the show when a huge theatre light came crashing down and landed not five centimetres away from me. There followed the collapse of the entire lighting and curtain rig, including heavy scaffolding, more large lights and thick black velvet curtains—all toppled down around me. The Comedy Festival SWAT emergency team, which until then I hadn't known existed, arrived within a minute: six burly men with dreadlocks, walkie-talkies, hammers, drills, power tools and ladders raced into the room and onto the stage. They immediately began reconstructing the set. I had no choice but to go and sit in the audience and improvise, using the time to introduce my mother and aunt to everyone. Mum was quiet but seemed to enjoy the attention—anything was better than having to watch her daughter do stand-up—although who ever knew for sure how she felt?

It is a cardinal rule during Comedy Festival time that, since there are so many shows in each venue, you must stick to your allotted sixty minutes. Consequently, because of all the mayhem, I didn't get time to do my Rage Against the Machine f-word spectacular, which led me to conclude that God had come to my rescue.

After the show Aunty Noreen congratulated me; Mum said nothing. This was absolutely the norm. Even when my mother came to see me in acceptable shows, such as the highly acclaimed Canadian hit *Mum's the Word*, which had no swearing (an extraordinary feat, given it was about child-birth and the rearing of small children), she would say nothing at all about them, as though the shows simply hadn't happened.

THE TOUR

I'm sure that if my father had lived to see my comedy, it would not have been such an issue between my mother and me. Dad would have loved what I did; he was that sort of dad. He wouldn't have noticed the swearing or the fact that jokes fell flat or that there were only five people in the audience. He would have brimmed with pride regardless, because it was his daughter standing up there on the stage. He could have been the buffer Mum needed. She could have come to see me perform and hidden her disapproval behind Dad's uninhibited, rapturous response.

But that wasn't to be. And so, early in my career, my mother and I came to an unspoken agreement: we would never talk about my comedy. We would pretend it didn't exist. While I childishly continued to crave her approval, my mother resolutely and stubbornly continued to withhold it.

It was a tension that sat between us always.

We never spoke of it.

Ever.

John in 1981 when I first met him

Together in our first show as the new Clown Ensemble (I'm wearing the bathing cap and John is in the striped cap)

chapter eleven

Post-awakening

From the moment I walked in our front door and announced, 'John, I think we should have sex more often' (whereupon John fainted and I had to slap him back to consciousness) it was obvious something of great importance had taken place on the tour of 2009. I realise there may be some eye rolling in response to my claim that what I experienced was an awakening. Those inclined to cynicism may even dismiss the event as nothing more than the consequence of a middle-aged woman drinking to excess. But, I put it to you, they'd be wrong.

I may well have been on all fours vomiting my guts out at the time, and in a state of trauma trying to get some confirmation as to whether I was twenty-four or fifty-four years of age while Gid and Stu resolutely refused to answer the question, but what happened to me that day on the road from Mount Spec to Townsville was an epiphany! Damn and blast it, that's what it was! How else do you describe a major turning point in life? I swear, from the moment I stood up I felt lighter—and not just because I had vomited so much. It was as though I'd been relieved of a heavy burden. I had a profound awareness that life is precious and wonderful and that more to the point we don't get long to experience it. I didn't want to waste any more time being negative and feeling shame. I wanted to be positive. I wanted to enjoy life. I wanted to celebrate and appreciate all that I had—John, kids, friends, family, work, two legs, two arms and one, albeit sun-damaged, head.

And, call it New Age mumbo jumbo, but it was at that moment by the roadside that I finally let go of trying to please my mother. Coincidentally, it was also the moment I stopped hating being a comedian and stopped hating myself.

I know. Wow!

For those of you feeling the urge to stick your fingers down your throat, I assure you I still adore the odd bit of negative thinking and am, as ever, prone to bouts of self-loathing and self-doubt, and thank God I am, because I think these are attributes that make for an interesting life. Put it this way: I'd rather have dinner with a cranky, crusty old borderline alcoholic than some happy-faced lentil-eating positive thinker on a liver-cleansing diet. It's just that I stopped those negative forces ruling my life.

My mum had actually stopped judging me a good five years before my 'awakening', her reservations about my work evaporating into thin air. She became content to just love me 'to bits' and, what was more, she was unafraid to show it, often beaming with unrestrained pride. This perhaps surprising change in attitude came about not so much through a moment of enlightenment but more because she developed Alzheimer's and completely forgot I was or ever had been a comedian, more often than not believing I was a nurse. It was one of the few positives during those nightmare Alzheimer's years.

In letting go of trying to please my mother I also inevitably let go, to some degree at least, of guilt. And, given that guilt goes hand in hand with having a parent with Alzheimer's, there was a lot of it. If my guilt were measured in oceanic terms it would have filled the Atlantic and Pacific and Indian oceans. Even Lake Eyre would have lost its tourist status, because it would have been full all the time.

Mostly, my guilt was to do with my mother living in a locked dementia unit. It was a sad fate and yet initially I had been upbeat about it. I thought the place Mum was in was marvellous. There was a joy and real commitment to giving the elderly residents' lives some purpose—singalongs, craft activities, bingo—they may not sound like reasons to live, but the residents were happy. Initially, my mum seemed to thrive: no longer having to live in the outside world with no memory was a huge relief to her. The staff were in the main brilliant, so caring, kind and dedicated to the residents, just as my mother had been back in her nursing days. But, like many of the 'caring sectors', aged-care facilities became victims of budget cuts, and so the yoga sessions, the music therapists, the massage therapists, the movement therapists, the Friday 'happy hour' with wine and beer, all disappeared.

And then there were the health regulations that meant my dog could no longer come into the unit with me. And smoking was banned from the patio area, and that really broke my heart, not because I smoked—I'd given up years earlier, as had my mother. The reason was because sitting outdoors on the patio with the carers and the few residents who did smoke had been fun; there was an almost festive atmosphere, and people both with and without dementia chatted and laughed together about their lives. Mum loved it; it was what she'd always done at her home—sit out the back of an evening and have a cup of tea and a smoke. But that became a thing of the past, and the facility was a sadder place for it. Even though the staff remained excellent throughout, I knew my mother deserved better—at the very least she deserved that I check out other accommodation possibilities; after all, I was her daughter, and she was relying on me to look after her. But I did nothing. I told myself my mum was in the best place for her needs, she was happy there, and it was close to my home, within walking distance, and that meant I could visit three times a week. The problem was that over the years the visits had dwindled to two, sometimes only one a week. Hence my ocean of guilt.

chapter twelve

Success is …

It wasn't as if all my guilt magically disappeared that day by the roadside outside Townsville, but I did cut myself some slack, told myself I was doing the best I could for my mother and that it was time to stop using her Alzheimer's, in the same way I had used my kids when they were young, as an excuse to avoid really going for it with my work. I needed to find out if, when I gave it my all, I could have a successful career.

I dreaded what could happen—what if I gave it my all and it turned out, as I'd suspected, that I really was a failure? The answer to that question came almost immediately. Within months of my return from the tour, my career, as they say in the trade, began to take off. One door opened, and then another, and then another …

One door opened onto the stage at the Comedy Theatre, and I got to fulfil my childhood dream: to stand alone there and perform my own solo show. It was called *Number 26*. There were people in the audience! A thousand people! And they'd even paid!

If you are to appreciate the following tale it is essential I describe my costume—a large, fluffy white dressing gown.

Underneath, I wore a high-cut black leotard and a pair of fish-net stockings, which the audience didn't see until the big reveal at the end of the show, when I performed a tap dance routine to the '131 008, silvertop taxis—why wait?' jingle. I've always been a firm believer in bringing home a show with a leotard—it can distract the audience from the fact that you haven't got a decent closing joke.

The first time I performed *Number 26* at the Comedy Theatre all was going well until my microphone stopped working. It was one of those tiny lapel mikes, the sort newsreaders wear clipped onto their jacket. It was attached by wires to a battery pack that was in turn attached to a belt that I wore under my leotard. When the battery went, not wanting to prematurely reveal the leotard I decided to leave the stage so the stage manager could change it in private. It wasn't ideal, but what could I do? I simply told the audience to talk among themselves; I'd be back soon.

A few minutes later, with a new battery in place, I stepped back onto the stage and continued with the show until the new battery stopped working. Like a brave soldier refusing to leave his mates at a time of crisis, I declared to my audience, 'I will not leave you again.' And so I stayed onstage. In the true spirit of showbiz, in order not to reveal the leotard, the poor manager—thankfully a woman—was forced to lie on the floor underneath me and virtually put her hand up my arse in order to change the battery.

With that mission successfully accomplished, once more I set forth, regaling the audience with stories of life with John and the kids at Number 26, until ten minutes later that battery died.

This time the stage manager had to admit that never in the history of the theatre had three battery packs died and that there was no other battery to be had, at which point she gave me a handheld microphone—the sort normally used by stand-ups. The problem was, this wasn't a stand-up show; it was more like a play. I'm not saying it was Shakespeare, but if you can imagine Juliet on the balcony saying, 'Romeo, Romeo, wherefore art thou, Romeo?' into a handheld mike, you get the idea. Not that I cared how odd it looked; nor did the audience. The important thing was they could hear me, and so on I went, mike in hand, until the battery in the handheld died.

For one mike to die was unfortunate. Two was unlucky. Three was unheard of. Four was downright spooky. I wondered if my unbridled excitement about being onstage at the Comedy was causing me to send out electrical frequencies so powerful that any technical equipment I came into contact with exploded under the pressure.

Mortified, the stage manager once more appeared, with the news that there was no other battery for the handheld. Rightio, then. I had no choice but to work without a microphone, and so I finished the show yelling my guts out. The leotard reveal worked a treat, and the audience seemed to appreciate the fact that they had seen my show as no other audience ever would.

While I was performing at the Comedy I was asked to audition for a new TV show called *Winners and Losers*, a 'dramedy'. I had no idea what a dramedy was, but it sounded impressive.

I'd already been called back three times to audition when my agent rang and said they wanted me to do a fourth. I asked him why.

'Scotty, they're just not sure if you know …'

'What?'

'… that you can act.'

Fair enough. At that stage I certainly had doubts.

This called for unprecedented action. I phoned Alan Brough, a man famous for the musical knowledge and quick wit he displayed every week on the much-loved TV show *Spicks and Specks*.

'Alan, I need your help.'

'What is it?'

'I need to learn to act.'

'You can already act, Ms Scott! I've seen you tell a comedian how much you loved their show after you'd just finished telling me how much you loathed it. It was a very convincing performance.'

'Maybe so, but I can't act at auditions.'

'Why not?'

'I guess I'm not used to it. I usually perform as myself, so having to act feels goosey.'

The next day Alan stood opposite me in my kitchen taking me through my paces. Naturally, I was playing the role I was auditioning for, Trish Gross, while Alan took the role of Jenny, my character's twenty-seven-year-old daughter. It was quite a dramatic piece. I had to express anger and disappointment and upset …

'Eye contact, Scotty, that's what acting is all about. Eye contact. No matter what, just keep looking at my eyes.'

It wasn't easy. Apart from the fact that I've always been uncomfortable holding anyone's gaze, Alan was 6 foot 5 to my 5 foot 2. By the end of the session my neck ached. But it worked. I got the job. To be cast in a TV part in my mid-fifties, while overweight, with irregular teeth, no botox, facial hair issues, warts and sun damage—as far as I was concerned this was a miracle right up there with Lazarus!

And, let me tell you, since then I have become quite the celebrity. I was in a public toilet standing in a long queue and at one point the woman in front of me said, 'Has anyone ever told you that you look like the actress in that show ...?'

That's the thing about us women in our fifties: we can never remember the name of a person, place, animal or thing, the miracle being that it doesn't matter—we understand one another perfectly anyway. And so without hesitation I replied to the woman, 'It *is* me. I'm Denise Scott, and I'm in *Winners and Losers*.'

This woman gasped in shock. 'Oh my God, you even sound like her.'

I said, 'That's because I *am* her. I'm Denise Scott.'

And then she said, 'You couldn't possibly be. Denise Scott is much fatter than you.'

I'm still in the process of deciding whether this was a compliment or an insult.

Getting the *Winners and Losers* gig was a high point, but I have to say that performing at the Langwarren Ladies Probus Club luncheon eclipsed it. It was a favour for my cousin's wife Wendy, whose grandma Bernis, in her role as president of the club, had requested me. I didn't get paid, of course, but Wendy, who kindly drove me to and from the gig, got fifty dollars petrol money.

I will never forget turning into the Probus Club car park to be greeted by seventy-eight-year-old Bernis, arms outstretched, legs wide apart, her president's medal, as big as a dinner plate, hanging on a ribbon around her neck. 'Thank God you've arrived, girls. I've been standing here for over half an hour saving a parking spot for you.' The fact that the car park was pretty near empty at the time was neither here nor there to a woman like Bernis.

The hall was full of women aged from their mid-fifties to their nineties. Bernis gestured towards an old lady in a wheelchair. 'Don't expect any laughs from her. She's as deaf as a doorpost, and her mind—it's completely gone, poor thing. Still, she enjoys a day out.'

We had lunch—roast beef and vegetables—and then Bernis introduced me as 'the greatest little comedian in Australia.'

The gig was going well when out of the blue I experienced a real-life senior moment: I couldn't for the life of me remember my closing joke. I could remember the set up: 'I'd like to leave you with a quote from one of the best motivational speakers I have ever heard. He said things like, "Success is ..."'

Nothing.

For years I'd finished with the same gag, must have said it a thousand times, but suddenly it was gone. Where there had once been a punchline was now an eternal expanse of blankness.

'Um, success is …'

More nothing.

'Success is …'

Again, nothing.

I had to confess. 'I'm really sorry about this, but, well, I always end my routine with the same story, but for some reason I've had a total blank. Sorry. Please bear with me. Success is …'

'Chocolate? Is it something to do with chocolate, Denise?'

I looked at the tiny white-haired lady who'd called out the suggestion. Her eyes sparkled. She was there to help, happy to help, dying to help.

As it turned out, every single woman in that room was there for me. They all understood, they all empathised, they all sympathised, and they were not going to let me down. For one of the first times in my life I truly understood the meaning of the term 'sisterhood'. I felt all those elderly women carrying me on their shoulders, and there was no way they were going to drop me.

'Good suggestion, thank you, but no, it's not chocolate. Success is …'

'Having all your own teeth?'

'Being able to change your radio setting from AM to FM?'

'Waking up in the morning and realising you haven't died?'

Those women were riotous. We laughed a lot, but after ten minutes I had to acknowledge defeat and admit I couldn't remember what the hell success was.

Five minutes later, as I sat with the ladies, chatting and eating dessert—tinned fruit salad and ice-cream—it came to me. 'I remember! I remember the end of my joke! Success is …'

All the women whooped and cheered as though I were a marathon runner who, after looking like she was never going to make it, had finally arrived in the Olympic stadium. They didn't care about hearing the end of my joke, because for them there was no greater success than someone forgetting something and then remembering it again.

Bernis stood up and thanked me for coming. She said she'd made a mistake in her introduction, because 'Denise Scott is not the best comedian in Australia. She is the best comedian in the WORLD!' Okay, it wasn't Dave Letterman or Stephen Colbert who made this observation, but it was Bernis; and she was the president of the Langwarren Ladies Probus Club, and that was enough to make my heart soar.

For those of you interested, success, according to that motivational speaker, was not about falling down; it was about falling down and getting back up again. And, even though I made a joke of it (and no, I'm not repeating the joke here—if you're that keen you can come and see me do it live), my awakening led me to agree. No matter what life throws at you, you must never give up. (Unless, in my case, I become allergic to wine, at which point I wouldn't see the point in living. After all, everyone has their limit.)

chapter thirteen

Rash behaviour

One day I went for a walk with my little dog, Raffi. As usual we headed towards the local shopping centre and suddenly, not five minutes from home, I saw a skin clinic. It featured a large photo of a beautiful woman in the window, all perfect teeth and dazzling, the best part being that this clinic promised that I too could look like that. I couldn't believe it. Surely this was a sign that the universe was looking out for me?

Months earlier, before going away on the 2009 tour, I'd attempted to do something about my skin by going to a skin specialist who, after peering at every mole, blemish and wart, declared there was nothing cancerous, so nothing to worry about.

'But what about the warts?'

'What about them?'

'Well, they don't look very nice.'

'No, they don't. Such a shame. I feel sorry for you, I really do. I mean to say, you could have them frozen off, but in your case where would one begin?'

'Well, what about this red rashy thing on my forehead?'

'Oh that? That's good old-fashioned sun damage.'

It was then that he suggested I grow a fringe, advice I had willingly heeded. But now here was a promise of beautiful flawless skin and so close to home! I tied Raffi to a lamp post out the front of the clinic and went inside.

I met Shana, who was extremely interested in my story and so sympathetic I could have wept with relief. She took me into a consulting room and asked me to pop my head inside a large box-shaped machine, a sort of X-ray kind of thing. (To be honest, I didn't understand what the hell it was.) Once my head was inside the box, I rested my chin on a small grooved shelf. Shana then asked me to close my eyes and wait for three flashes of blue light.

Three flashes of blue light later I emerged from the box, and Shana explained that the images of my face were now travelling to her laptop computer, which was sitting in front of her on the desk. 'And I have to warn you, Denise: the images are designed to show every single imperfection you have, so you might be a little shocked …'

The laptop whirred into life and suddenly there I was, in three infra-red images of my face taken from three different angles. Shocked was an understatement. Suicidal would have been more on the money. Not only were all my blemishes and wrinkles and circles under my eyes highlighted as though with thick black texta, but there were thousands and thousands of tiny white spots the size of a pin head covering my entire face.

'They're blackheads, Denise. And you see here, and here?' I nodded feebly. 'Well, that's where you have blackheads on your sunspots.' Oh my God. I thought I was going to faint. 'But don't worry; we can eliminate all those flaws.'

Shana produced a piece of paper on which was printed a simple outline of a face, neck and shoulders. With the aid of a black biro she busied herself covering the face with squiggles. She then turned the paper to face me and explained all the problem areas, which appeared to be my entire face. She discussed the various treatments and procedures I needed to undergo. When she had finished, she asked, 'How does that sound, Denise?'

'It sounds great, Shana, but how much will it cost?'

Once more Shana went to town with her biro and paper, squiggling figures down the right-hand side of the page with an intensity and focus that bordered on ferocious. Finally, she turned the paper towards me.

I stared at it for some time. 'I'm sorry, Shana, but which one of these figures is the actual cost?'

She tapped her French-manicured nail on a number.

Had I been a cartoon character my eyes would have *boi-oi-oinged* out of their sockets, and steam would have come out of my ears, and my body would have blasted out of the chair and shot through the roof, flown through the sky, whizzed around the universe a couple of times, hurtled back to earth, crashed back into the skin clinic, and, as my dust-covered head poked up through the hole in the floorboards, I would have said, in a funny Mickey Mouse kind of voice, 'Nine thousand, four hundred and seventy-five dollars?'

'I know it sounds like a lot, but there is a lot of work that needs to be done. But you're lucky, because for this week only we're offering a twenty per cent discount to all clients who pay the total fee upfront! This means …' Shana produced a calculator and manically pressed buttons, 'that you only have to spend seven thousand, five hundred and eighty dollars!'

I looked at my white-spotted infra-red face staring at me from the computer screen and whimpered, 'When could we start?'

'Let's see …' Shana looked at her calendar. 'Denise, it's your lucky day. We've had a cancellation. I can see you at five o'clock tomorrow. Do you want to pay the full amount now?'

I explained I couldn't do that because I didn't have a credit card. I promised to return the next day with a cheque.

The next day I took Raffi for another walk to the shops, but this time in the opposite direction. I was in a state of high anxiety. My stomach was knotted; I hadn't slept. To spend nearly ten thousand dollars on my skin … But then again, if it worked and I didn't have to feel embarrassed any more … But what if it didn't work? No, bugger it, I needed to do something … And that was when the universe arrived to rescue me in the form of Kerry Eccles.

Kerry was an old friend who lived in the 'hood. She was sitting at a table outside the Book Grocer. She invited me to join her in a coffee.

I told her my skin clinic story.

'Crock of shit.' Kerry said it with no hesitation. 'I tell you, Scotty, it's an absolutely diabolical, disgusting crock of shit. If you go ahead with … with whatever it's called, I'm going to have to get a few of my big old lezzo girlfriends to come around and damn well tie you up and sit on top of you and slap you until you come to your senses.' Kerry had always been an opinionated woman and had become even more so since suffering a stroke in her forties. 'Scotty, only last week I saw you on the TV, on that show, what's it called? You know, that panel show, with what's-his-name hosting, and you were sitting next to that gorgeous little slip of a thing, oh, you know, she's that singer, or is she an actress? Anyway, I saw you sitting there on that show, Scotty, and do you know what I thought? I thought, Gee, that Scotty scrubs up well. That's what I thought, and sitting here with you now do you know what I see?'

Not much, I thought, given that since her stroke Kerry had been pretty close to blind.

She took a deep, lusty suck on her cigarette and lifted her sunglasses. 'I see a face that's in really good shape. All you need is a holiday in Bali and a jar of bloody good moisturiser.'

I went home via a chemist, bought a nice moisturiser and cancelled my appointment at the skin clinic.

John and I together at a friend's wedding (we never married)

chapter fourteen

Chook meet

Soon after returning from the 2009 tour, completely out of the blue, I received a call from my old school friend Jay-O. I hadn't spoken to her in years. 'Hi, Scott,' she said. (Jay-O always called me Scott, never Scotty.) 'I'm having a chook meet at my place and need some entertainment, and I think you'd be perfect.'

Okay, it wasn't exactly Hollywood, but it was an amazing offer, especially since my knowledge of poultry was, quite frankly, paltry. Boom-boom!

Jay-O lived in St Andrews, north-east of Melbourne. Her home had survived the Black Saturday bushfires, but many in her community and surrounding area had not been so fortunate. There were those who had lost homes, livelihoods, pets and, most devastating of all, family. A few had lost their entire family. Jay-O had wanted to do something to lift the spirits of her grieving community, so she had gone to all the fire-recovery centres and put up notices asking if anyone was interested in getting together and knitting chooks. The idea had taken off, and, before you could say 'Knit one, purl one, pass the slip stitch over' there were groups of women gathering together in fire-recovery centres, portable rooms and makeshift homes, creating through their loss, all with a common aim: to knit a chook! Eventually, it was decided to celebrate their creations, and thus the chook meet.

'We're going to have all the chooks on display and there's going to be a real chook judge. And I thought these people had been through so much, Scott, they could really do with a laugh.' I agreed. 'But Scott, I don't want anyone to know who the entertainment is going to be, so if it's okay with you, all I'm going to put on the poster is "Surprise celebrity guest."'

Oh dear. I might have had an epiphany, but, as already mentioned, I still had enough self-doubt to immediately picture Jay-O introducing me on the night: 'And now, ladies and gentlemen, for our surprise celebrity guest, make welcome Denise Scott!' at which point there'd be a sea of quizzical faces all asking the same question: Denise who?

John drove me to St Andrews on the night of the chook meet. It was eerie. Even though it was nightfall and for the most part the main road seemed to have been unaffected by the fires, you could sense the devastation nearby. Small details—a smoke-stained street sign, a burnt-out tree—were enough to hint at the horror that had filled that day.

'I feel sick, John ...'

'About the fires?'

'No.' (Honestly, sometimes John could be so far off the mark.) 'About me, having to perform tonight. What am I going to do? I can't just do my normal shtick.'

'Why not?'

'Because, John, call me crazy, but I don't think doing a routine about how hard it is to have G-cup breasts is appropriate for people who've just lost everything in a fire.'

'Scotty, it'll be great. People love big breast stuff.'

'Oh God, John ... And did I tell you that Jay-O said there's a rumour been going round, and do you know who everyone thinks the surprise guest is going to be?'

'Who?'

'Ian Smith.'

'Who's Ian Smith?'

'Harold Bishop!'

'Who?'

'Harold from *Neighbours*. You know—the old guy with glasses who plays the tuba and he disappeared at sea in one episode and came back five years later having suffered amnesia. Anyway, that's who they're expecting to be at the chook meet.'

'So? They'll be getting you!'

'My point exactly! Haven't these people already suffered enough? And now all they want is to see Harold Bishop and it's going to be me, oh ...' I groaned.

About 2 kilometres from Jay-O's place we turned onto a dirt road; by now it was pitch black. A chap in a fluoro jacket waved a torch at us. John stopped and wound down his window.

'Goin' to the chook meet, are youse?'

'Yes, we are.'

'Well, let me tell ya, mate, it's bigger than bloody Woodstock up there.' I felt ill. 'Yeah, so we can't let any more cars through, so youse are gonna have t' park here and walk in. Youse got a torch?'

'No, we haven't.'

'Well, be bloody careful. There's a few potholes.'

John and I held hands. At one point I stumbled.

'You alright, Scotty?'

'Yeah, it's just my ankle. Geez, arthritis gives me the shits.'

And then I recalled why we were there, and John and I continued our journey in respectful silence.

'Oh, Scott, thank you so much for coming.' Jay-O hugged us both. I was blown away. She had always been a stunner at school, but to see her that night, looking pretty much the same, was, quite frankly, upsetting. She still had smooth olive skin, not a wrinkle in sight; her teeth were so white and straight, her cheekbones high and her hair wild and curly— she looked no more than thirty. Surely she'd had work done! But sadly I knew that wasn't the case. She radiated love and contentment and peace.

Her husband, Ronnie, also had the whole 'beauty within, beauty without' business going on. He'd built their mudbrick house twenty-eight years earlier. It featured high ceilings, beautiful artworks, a large rustic kitchen and in the bathroom a ceiling-to-floor window that allowed you your own private view of the bush as you lay in the sunken bath.

The place was packed with hundreds of people, and, as naive as it sounds, I wasn't prepared for what I encountered. Everywhere I looked I saw a face that was grief-stricken and sad beyond comprehension, haunted by the events of that dreadful day. What had I been expecting? That people would be laughing and chatting and having a good old party time? I guess that was exactly what I had been expecting.

I walked into the main living area and had I followed my instincts I would have burst into tears. The room was full of knitted chooks—ninety-three of them. They all had such presence and dignity, proudly sitting up on hay bales and shelves, in nests that had been lovingly placed all around the room. There were fat and skinny hens, a mother hen with a brood of chicks; some were adorned with knitted jewels, some with knitted hats. What struck me was their overwhelming beauty. Even the one that looked disabled—its cockscomb, instead of being on top of its head, was coming out the side of its neck—was adorable and had indeed won the Chook with the Best Personality award. I noted there was a cock, just the one—a great relief, because as a comedian I didn't see a cock; I saw a joke. But then Jay-O informed me that the knitter of this chook had lost everything in the fires, and I thought, No, I won't make fun of it. Then I thought, But I am desperate—so maybe …

Because I was desperate. Big breasts aside, what on earth could I say to these people to make them laugh?

Jay-O introduced me to one of the locals. 'Mary, this is Denise.'

'Hello, nice to meet you, Denise. Have you knitted a chook?'

Jay-O whispered conspiratorially, 'No, Denise Scott. She's the surprise guest.'

'Oh! I thought it was going to be Harold Bishop.'

Oh God, kill me now.

Jay-O called everyone to attention. Some people gathered in the living area, while those who couldn't fit inside remained outside, looking through the large windows. Ronnie had organised an excellent PA system, so everyone could hear. As Jay-O introduced me, she recalled that it was thanks to me that she had met Ronnie.

What? Was it? In keeping with the theme of the night, my mind quickly unravelled like a ball of wool, and went back in time until there I was, sixteen years old, dancing at Bushbeat. Of course! I'd taken Jay-O with me to the Friday night dances at Eltham High School, and consequently she'd met Ronnie and they'd lived in blissful happiness ever since.

There was warm applause as I stepped onto the stage—a magnificent wooden coffee table handmade by Ronnie. Initially, I had insisted to Jay-O that it would break if I stood on it, but Jay-O had been equally insistent that it wouldn't. I have never in my performing career reached the point at which I've had the microphone actually in my hand and still had no idea what I'm going to say. That night, though, I came close. As I stepped with great reluctance onto the table, I had nothing. And then it came to me. Of course! Bushbeat! Eltham was close enough to St Andrews, and the audience was close enough to my age, that maybe they had also attended those dances. And so I told the story of how I'd pashed Robbie Buckle even though his mouth had been full of vomit. The audience laughed, which was gratifying, but there followed a great deal of whispering.

'Is something wrong?' I said.

A woman at the back of the room put her hand up. 'Denise, I pashed Robbie Buckle, too.'

And then another hand went up and a woman said, 'So did I.'

And then another hand went up and another woman said, 'So did I.'

And then a woman stood up and proudly declared, 'Well, I had *sex* with Robbie Buckle.'

And then another woman stood up and said, 'So did I.'

And then a man stood up and said, 'So did I!'

And suddenly the people who had been so grim faced and shell-shocked and sad were laughing and beaming, united in the fact that nearly everyone there, it seemed, apart from me, had had sex with Robbie Buckle.

It was a miracle. I couldn't believe that nearly forty years after that kiss Robbie had arrived like a knight in shining armour and rescued me in my hour of need.

After my performance I asked one of the women what the sex with Robbie had been like. She looked into the distance all dreamy eyed and beamed, 'Denise, it was awesome.'

A month or so after the chook meet I was being interviewed on radio by Waleed Aly when, apropos of nothing, he asked, 'So, Denise, any regrets?'

Yes. Not fucking Robbie Buckle when I was sixteen.

That was my exact thought, so instant and clear that for one ghastly second I thought I'd actually said the words out loud, which would have been tricky given I was on ABC Radio at the time. Nevertheless, I was shocked by the thought. Since when had I regretted not having sex with Robbie Buckle? And, more to the point, since when had I started using the f-word as a verb? Who did I think I was? Kim Cattrall in an episode of *Sex and the City*?

'Denise?'

'Oh, yes, sorry Waleed, vagued out there for a second; you were asking?'

'If you had any regrets.'

'Yes, I do. I very much regret not being able to play the ukulele.'

To go from sex to ukulele in less than five seconds was for my money nothing short of genius. And the ukulele regret was even true. I explained to Waleed that my mother was living in a locked dementia unit and how difficult it could be to have a conversation with someone with Alzheimer's. I recalled once asking my mother, 'How are you going, Mum?' to which she replied, 'I'm as good as gold.' Then she looked at me and said, 'And what about your mother? How is she going?'

It was an awkward moment. I had replied, 'She's as good as gold, apparently; at least, that's what I've been told.'

John, on the other hand, could simply stand in the middle of the crowded dining room in the dementia unit and start playing his ukulele: the sheer joy and sense of calm it brought to all the residents was nothing short of a miracle. On one memorable occasion, a resident named Sheila called out to John, 'Do you know "I belong to Glasgow"?' John didn't know it, but that was no problem for Sheila, who began to belt it out regardless. One by one the residents joined in until they were all singing their hearts out, faces beaming. John managed to play along. Finally, they finished the song.

Not two seconds later Sheila looked at John and said, 'Do you know "I belong to Glasgow"? It's one of my favourite songs, and I haven't heard it in years.'

And so John played it again … and again…

Waleed then did a spiel about there being no point going through life with regrets and made me promise that I would learn to play the ukulele and perform a song onstage, an empty promise if ever there was one.

A few days later I had dinner with my good buddy Fran. I told her the whole story, about the chook meet, Waleed, my regret.

She looked puzzled. 'But why do you regret not having sex with Robbie Buckle?'

'Because I think it would have been awesome. And I really believe that if I'd had a simple, uncomplicated, straightforward, hot introduction to sex, no strings attached, as opposed to … well … as opposed to the one I did have—not that it was bad, it was great; well, I assume it was; I actually can't remember it in any detail, and then the relationship that followed was so messy—I would have grown up to be a happier, better adjusted human being.'

Fran looked unconvinced, but nevertheless offered the following words of wisdom: 'I went to school with a girl whose mother often used to say, "You must never go through life regretting not sleeping with someone."' Right on, sister!

'Yeah, she ended up sleeping with her daughter's husband.' Not so right on.

In early 2010 I joined Facebook because I thought it important to know what four thousand of my closest friends were going to have on their sandwich for lunch. One day I went online to discover that a friend of a friend of a friend of a friend—a woman—had sent me a photo. It was a picture of a man standing in his laundry, casually leaning against his top-load washing machine. He was totally bald, had a large handlebar moustache, an enormous beer gut and was wearing a mankini, which led me to conclude that all his clothes must have been in the wash. He had a large Laughing Buddha tattoo on his stomach and was holding a can of Jim Beam.

There was no message and no name. I stared at the photo, wondering why this friend of a friend of a friend of a friend had forwarded it to me. I peered at this bald man's face; it sure as hell beat peering at his gut.

And then I saw it—the sparkle in his eyes.

It was Robbie Buckle.

Did I still regret not having sex with him when I was sixteen? Not so much. It felt as though life had come full circle—from a vomit-mouthed kiss to a photo on Facebook via a chook meet in St Andrews.

chapter fifteen

Comedy and death

On a Monday evening late in March 2011 I performed at the Palais Theatre as part of the opening-night gala of the Melbourne International Comedy Festival. Later that night, when I arrived home and John asked me how I'd gone in my three and a half minutes onstage, I confidently replied, 'Pretty good. In fact, I reckon it was my best gala yet!'

A few days later, the following Thursday to be precise, I was on location for *Winners and Losers* filming a hospital scene; my onscreen character, Trish Gross, had been diagnosed with breast cancer. We wrapped at 6.15 pm and immediately I jumped in a cab and headed into the city. It was the opening night of my new show, *Regrets*, which was based on Robbie Buckle, the chook meet and the Facebook photo. For the next month I was going to perform it every night except Mondays.

On that first night, I had an hour to kill before curtain time, so I headed to the Westin Hotel. It was a showbiz trick I'd learnt years earlier—to go to a swish hotel and set up camp in their lounge area. I sat down in a comfy leather armchair and ordered a pot of tea from the stylish waiter. I didn't want tea, but I saw the eight dollars fifty—that was how much an Earl Grey cost in that establishment—as cheap rent for an upmarket space where I could sit, collect my thoughts and rehearse my show. How does one rehearse a solo show while sitting in a bar? Simple! One sits there drinking tea and talking to oneself. It's quite marvellous. No-one comes near you.

After finishing my run-through I headed to the ladies, where I changed into my stage outfit—a funky animal-print dress with a sheer black jacket. I applied make-up and then proceeded, in my orthotic runners, to walk to the nearby Victoria Hotel, in which my performance venue was located.

While it may not have had the sophistication of the Westin I was nevertheless happy to be performing at the Victoria Hotel. Every night when I walked into the foyer I marvelled anew at the wide marble staircase that swept up to the first-floor bar. Covered in worn carpet, it still managed to maintain a quiet dignity, a downmarket grandeur, and I respected that quality—I'd even go so far as to say I related to it. I also loved how behind the reception desk a holland blind (of correct dimensions) was pulled down to cover the enormous fish tank, thus enabling the fish to get a good night's sleep while comedy fans poured in and out of the building.

I was nervous and avoided speaking to any of the other comics in the foyer; instead, I headed downstairs to my venue, a conference room that had been converted into a temporary theatre courtesy of a makeshift stage, raked seating and a light-ing rig, all hired for the occasion. I stood backstage. It didn't quite have the dignity of the staircase. In a word, it was putrid. I did some deep-breathing exercises, raising my arms on the *in* breath, lowering them again on the *out* breath.

In …

Out.

In …

Out.

Jesus Christ, what was that smell? The place stank.

Urine! That was it. Stinking stale urine. This tiny back room had more than likely been used as a urinal; it wasn't as if there was a toilet backstage, and once the audience came in there was no way out. Ah, the joys of being a showbiz celebrity.

Dori, my stage manager and tech, put on my house music—motown hits that had been rejigged to have a contemporary sound. It was my solution to being old but wanting to appear to be a happening human being still in touch with modern-day life. I swapped my orthotic runners for a pair of high heels.

I did the show. I spoke about my regrets, including not being able to play the ukulele and not having had sex with Robbie Buckle. At the end of the show I played 'I belong to Glasgow' on the ukulele. This had nothing to do with keeping my promise to Waleed Aly and everything to do with the reality that, though not quite as effective as wearing a leotard, playing the ukulele badly also distracts an audience from noticing that you don't have a decent gag to finish your show. The audience ticked all the boxes—they came, they stayed, they laughed, they applauded, they left in an apparent state of happiness. I was relieved and just a little bit pleased with myself. It was going to be a great festival.

It was early the following Sunday morning when the call came from the dementia unit. My mother was unwell. She went to hospital to have an X-ray. The doctors thought it was constipation, but it wasn't. The next day Mum was diagnosed with advanced ovarian cancer. My sister and I made it clear there was to be no treatment, only pain relief.

That evening the Comedy Festival gala screened on TV. And then all hell broke loose. My Facebook page was swamped with posts of the negative kind. It appeared that in my 'pretty good' comedy spot I had managed to offend alcoholics, coeliacs and people with Asperger's—one hell of a trifecta.

From the alcoholics there was only one complaint, and being a borderline alcoholic myself I liked to think I had a right to say whatever I wanted. As for the coeliacs, at the risk of causing more offence, I didn't care if I did upset them. Not one bit. So what if they couldn't eat wheat? Honestly, get a grip, people! What did make me feel sick to my stomach, though, was that people believed I'd made jokes at the expense of children with Asperger's. As I said in my online apology, why would I joke about something like that? I don't find it funny.

My joke had been about people who *claimed* to be alcoholic or coeliac or to have mild Asperger's when in reality they didn't and just used the label as an excuse for bad behaviour. Sadly, the nub of my joke appeared to have become somewhat lost in translation. I hoped my sincere and heartfelt apology would be the end of it.

Meanwhile, I went to the hospital to sit with my mother. She was distressed. 'Why are you doing this to me, Denise?'

'What, Mum?'

'Keeping me prisoner.'

'Mum, I'm not keeping you prisoner. You're in hospital. You're not well.'

'Oh Denise, please don't lie to me.'

'I'm not lying, Mum. You're quite ill.'

'How would you know what the hell I am?'

'Because I just do.'

'Oh, that'd be right. You always were the one who knew everything.'

My stomach knotted. I reminded myself that my mother had Alzheimer's.

Her anxiety continued. 'Denise, please, you've got to get me out of here.'

'I can't, Mum. Not now. Perhaps in another hour, after you've seen the doctor,' I lied.

'I don't need to see a bloody doctor. If you don't do something, I'll just get up and walk out of here myself and you'll never see me again.'

My mother said 'bloody'? This was serious.

Later that afternoon my sister arrived and I went to the hospital canteen for a break. My mobile rang. It was Kev, my manager. I sensed my day was not about to get any better. 'Hi, Scotty, how's your mum?'

'Still alive—that's about all I can say.'

'Yeah, well, I'm sorry, Scotty, but I thought I'd better ring and let you know the *Herald Sun* are probably going to run the story tomorrow.'

'Oh Jesus.'

'Yeah, I did my best. I tried to talk the journo out of it. To be honest, I used your mother's situation, but unfortunately no dice. I've pushed him to print your apology but he wasn't sure.'

'Oh God.'

'And I have to tell you I've had people from various autism groups on the phone, and they're pretty upset …' How I wanted to run and hide. The familiar sense of shame was crackling, preparing to make a big, incendiary comeback. 'I think it's because these people have such stressful lives, you know, with all they have to deal with, and they've just got to vent somehow.'

I said nothing.

'Anyway, Scotty, I just wanted to give you the heads up.'

That night, my sister and a group of her friends came to see the show—an arrangement that had been made before Mum's hospitalisation. Jay-O and Ronnie along with a large group of people from the chook meet were also in the audience. Included in their posse was one of the many who, as an adolescent, had had sex with Robbie Buckle. I spoke to her during the show, and she informed the entire audience that the love tryst had taken place down an old mine shaft.

'And was it awesome?'

'Actually, it was pretty ordinary.'

Afterwards, we all had a drink together and I took comfort in their company.

Meanwhile, John had gone straight from work to the hospital to sit with Mum. He informed me later that they had watched *Winners and Losers* together, and Mum had appeared to enjoy it.

'Did she know it was me in the show?'

'I don't think so.'

'Oh, well, that would be why she enjoyed it.'

As predicted, the next day the article appeared in the *Herald Sun*. Kev rang me early that morning. I was already at the hospital and took the call in the foyer. Although my online apology had been included in the article it seemed it hadn't quite cut the mustard … 'If it's any comfort, Scotty, the whole thing will have blown over in three days max. But for now, you'd better prepare yourself because every nutter in the fucking country is going to jump online and have their say. I suggest you don't go anywhere near a computer for a few days, and please, don't, whatever you do, look at the *Herald Sun* online forum. I've just checked it and it's ugly.' I felt as though a medicine ball was being thrown at my guts over and over again. 'Yeah, the timing is awful, but I swear, for two or three days it'll spread like wildfire, and then it will run out of oxygen and disappear. Oh, and I should warn you, I've got messages here from other media.'

'You're kidding?'

'I wish I was, but if you don't mind I'm going to go in hard and really play the dying mother card.'

'Please play it. I mean to say, it's the truth—my mother is dying and I just need to be with her. I can't be dealing with this other stuff, not now.'

I went back to the ward and resumed my vigil. Even though my mother needed to be in palliative care she was still stuck in a surgical ward—something to do with the bureaucratic process. This meant that numerous times throughout the day surgeons, always accompanied by a gaggle of student doctors, would gather around my mother's bed. They'd ask her questions, and each time she would become abusive, and I would have to explain she had Alzheimer's and endlessly repeat that 'no, my mother is not going to have surgery.'

As the days wore on my mother's anxiety escalated to fury. 'Denise, why? Why are you doing this to me? For God's sake, I'm your mother. How could you be so cruel? As soon as I get out of here I swear I'll never have anything to do with you again.'

'Denise Scott?' I recognised Geraldine immediately. I had gone to school with her, both primary and secondary. 'I saw there was a Margaret Scott in this ward and thought it might be your mum.' Geraldine explained that she had worked as a nurse at the hospital for thirty-six years and was now …

Her voice faded. I was no longer listening; I was too busy having a religious experience. I saw a glowing golden halo surrounding Geraldine's head and I heard an angelic choir singing the Hallelujah Chorus and I knew without a skerrick of doubt that she was our ticket for getting Mum out of the surgical ward and into palliative care.

I told her of our plight, and for some reason (a comedian's constant state of self-absorption, perhaps?) I went on to regale her with the story of the autism business and then dared to ask, 'Were you by any chance at the school centenary dinner?'

'No I wasn't, Scotty,' and here she gave me a meaningful look, 'but I heard all about it.'

'Oh,' I groaned.

In turn Geraldine told me she had followed my career because her mother, a conservative, deeply religious, straight-shooting eighty-four-year-old Catholic woman, had kept a scrapbook of my work. 'She's so proud of you, Denise. She brings out the scrapbook all the time. Bores us stupid with it.'

I was taken aback. How come Geraldine's mother was proud of me when my own mother …? Ah, but of course, Geraldine's mother could feel proud of me because I wasn't her daughter!

That afternoon my sister and I tag-teamed—Julie took up residence in the chair next to Mum's bed while I went home. Stupidly, I checked my Facebook page. A lynch mob had gathered. Its numbers were few, but the vitriol was gobsmacking. I noticed that an 'I hate Denise Scott' page had been created. Some were calling for my death—at least, I assumed that was what they meant by 'BURN! BURN! BURN!'

That evening I was early for my show so went and grabbed a coffee at a small cafe in nearby Swanston Street. I gazed out the window and watched people hurrying to and fro on their way home from work or out to dinner, and I felt a distinct pang of envy.

I envied their ordinariness.

I longed for the day my life would feel normal again. I pondered the synchronicity of the two major events happening in my life—my mother dying and the online hate campaign inspired by my work as a comedian. Mother versus comedy—that old chestnut! Once more the battle was raging. The resulting tension was crippling. While my heart was pulling towards my mother, my bruised ego was pulling towards my career. I was dismayed that at the end of my mother's life I was still finding time to worry about my work. It felt like an enormous betrayal.

In the foyer of the Vic I kept my eyes down and spoke to no-one. In my venue, Dori, my tech, gave me a warm hug, which I appreciated. I went and peeked through the curtains and watched the audience coming in. I imagined that there was someone with a gun who halfway through my show would stand up and cry, 'Not funny!' and shoot me dead. A vitriolic online hate campaign can make a girl think that way.

The music faded, the house lights went down, I took a deep breath and walked to the middle of the stage. I had never felt so alone in my life.

Words came out of my mouth, but I had no connection with them. I was sure the audience was looking at me as though I was insane, because without doubt I was kind of mentally unwell. I was too hot and felt faint. I was thinking, I have to tell the audience I'm not feeling well, say I'm sorry but I can't continue. But then I told myself that the show must go on.

By the end of the show I was having an out-of-body experience. Of course, I'd had one before—at the Our Lady of Mercy centenary dinner—but this was much worse. I was looking down at myself struggling to deliver my jokes, getting everything mixed up; sentences and punchlines were coming out all wrong. I made it to the end but left the stage feeling devastated. I'd let the audience down. I'd let myself down.

The following evening I cancelled my show. I ate a nourishing dinner and had some wine. John checked my Facebook page for me—something we'd agreed he would do while the hate campaign continued—and announced with a beaming smile that, yes, there were still lots of abusive posts, but there were also 'lots of nice posts from people supporting you, and there's even some guy campaigning to get the "I hate Denise Scott" page shut down.' Positive or negative, the fact that people were warring about me on Facebook made me feel ill. I had learnt a lesson, that was for sure: when Facebook is good, it's very good, but when it's bad, it's soul destroying. I took a sleeping tablet and went to bed.

A day later I filmed some scenes for *Winners and Losers*, and such is the wonder of TV that all it took was for someone to ask my character, 'So, Trish, how's the cancer?' and for me to reply, 'It's all clear,' and bingo! The drama was over, and we moved on to a sexier storyline involving the young characters in the show. If only real life could be that straightforward.

Thanks to Saint Geraldine, my mother was moved to the palliative-care unit. What was immediately striking upon arrival was the overwhelming sense of peace and calm—as though, finally, after an epic and difficult journey, we'd made it home.

Initially, Mum was sharing a room, but two days after our arrival she was moved to a private room. We knew what this meant. The palliative-care nurses were always moving patients, making sure that when their time came they and their family had privacy. My mother was lapsing in and out of consciousness. Family members started to visit. Once more I cancelled my show. My sister, John and I prepared ourselves for the long night ahead.

THE TOUR

As I sat by my mother's side I pondered the silence in the unit. Mum had been there nearly three days, and in that time who knew how many other patients had died? Three, four? Maybe more. And yet at no point had there been any noise. No loud wailing, no sobs, not even the sound of subdued tears: just a beautiful quiet peacefulness, as though everyone understood we were there for the same purpose—to die or to farewell someone who was dying. And so out of respect for all those who had to share this space, people went about the business of saying goodbye with an exquisite, delicate silence. It was humanity at its very best. It was as though everything rotten about life had been stripped away, and all that remained was love, a very pure sense of love.

I contemplated the synchronicity of events again, but this time rather than seeing the timing of the Facebook hate campaign as 'unfortunate', I felt that there could have been no better time for it, because being inside the palliative-care unit I felt protected from the outside world. No-one could hurt me. I was in an oasis of calm. To my surprise, I let go of all the work stuff; it had no relevance any more. There were bigger, more important things to think about, such as life and death, and love, and family. I went so far as to wonder whether my mother, in her own weird and wonderful way, even in death, was looking out for me. It was a long bow to draw, but I liked the idea.

In the communal kitchen, I bumped into a woman who looked younger than me and recognised her as the mother of the young man in the room next to my mum's, who had cancer of the throat. She was there day and night, blending food that she fed him via a tube. It broke my heart when, as we stood side by side washing dishes, this woman asked what had brought me there. I felt guilty as I explained it was my mother, who, at eighty-six years of age, having lived with Alzheimer's for over ten years, had been diagnosed with cancer.

'Oh, I'm so sorry,' the mother of the young man said, with genuine concern.

My mother had lived her life, but as for this woman's son … I smiled gratefully and said nothing.

Julie and I attempted to sleep on the fold-out bed in Mum's room, but it was impossible. John set up camp in the communal lounge area, lying on the couch, his head on a cushion, a jacket covering his eyes to shade them from the glare of the streetlight coming in through the window.

The peace I had earlier been lulled into was replaced with a new tension: death was on its way, but when? And what would it be like? Did I want to witness it? I wanted to be there with my mother, that was for sure, but I was scared. I'd never seen death before.

As the hours ticked by, the fear of facing Mum's death changed to impatience. Now I wanted death to come. I was sick of waiting. I wanted it to be over. I wanted my mother to be out of pain, to be liberated from her Alzheimer's. *I* wanted to be liberated from her Alzheimer's, from having to worry about her. I wanted to be liberated from guilt. I was not proud to feel this way.

At 4 am Mum stirred. Julie and I stood on either side of the bed. After two days of barely being conscious she was trying to speak. We leant in. 'What is it, Mum? What do you want to say?' She muttered something but we couldn't hear. We moved closer. 'What is it, Mum?'

'I'm angry.'

Just to make sure I'd heard correctly I bent even further over her and said, 'Pardon, Mum?'

'I said I'm angry!'

'Who are you angry with, Mum?'

'I'm angry with the whole world.'

My sister and I looked at each other, then at Mum, and then at each other again. Angry with the whole world? God Almighty, how the hell was Mum going to achieve peace before dying now?

Our mother started to talk about the nuns who had taught her at primary school. 'They thought they were so holy, they thought they knew me, but they didn't have a clue what was going on.' She also referred to the adults who, when she was little, had called her 'the bastard'. She kept asking, 'Will they be there? I don't want to see them.'

By this stage, Mum wasn't the only one who was angry. My sister was also angry. So was I.

I was angry because my mother was angry, and I was devastated that she might die angry. I wanted to say, 'For God's sake, Mum, why the hell didn't you do something about this years ago, get some counselling? There's nothing any of us can do about it now.' I was angry that Mum's 'secret', which wasn't even a secret any more—everybody knew about it; it was just that no-one ever spoke of it—still held so much power. I wanted to tell her that it wasn't just about her. Given the circumstances, I admit this was a little harsh—surely, if ever there's a time when it should be all about you, it's when you are about to pass from this world to the next. But it did feel as though it wasn't just about Mum: it was also about my grandmother May and my sister and me. May could have been in the room with us: four angry women raging against this stupid secret and the subsequent shame and belief that no matter what we did in life we were never good enough. For eighty-six years it had held pride of place in our family. Eighty-six years! I think I can safely say I was speaking for all of us when I muttered quietly, 'I'm so over this.'

A nurse came in—her lilting Irish accent a little too bright and bubbly for my liking. She checked my mother's pulse and asked her how she was doing.

My mother answered that she would like a cup of tea.

'It's a miracle!' The nurse looked at us, her face beaming, her eyes misty, then turned and looked upwards to heaven as though she'd just seen a vision of the Virgin Mary. 'It happens sometimes at the end. They rally and come back for a while; they're just not ready to go. Aren't you girls lucky?'

I looked at that nurse with as much dismay as I have ever felt in my life. Lucky? Was she kidding? There was nothing lucky about this.

Eventually, Julie, John and I went home to grab a couple of hours' sleep, leaving Mum to enjoy some jelly.

A few hours later I returned to the hospital and had a meeting with the doctor, who explained that it could be another week or two, even three …

My dilemma was that I still had two more weeks of Comedy Festival shows at night, and filming for series one of *Winners and*

Losers was scheduled to finish in a few days' time, at which point we were going to break for some months. I was needed for a big doozy affair—Bec and Matt's wedding—with a cast of hundreds. While I didn't have much to say or do, it was essential for me to be there for it. If I couldn't get there it would mean that hundreds of people would be unable to work, and cast and crew would have to change their holiday arrangements. What was I to do?

The doctor looked at me with sympathy. She asked if I was close to my mother.

I replied in the affirmative.

Had I spent much time with her in the previous years?

Affirmative.

Did I trust the staff at the palliative-care unit?

Affirmative.

She explained that often it was those family members who hadn't spent much time with their ailing relative who needed to be there when they died, to appease guilt and make up for lost time. In my case she suggested that for now I should go on with my life and see what happened.

If ever the expression 'a new day dawns' was apt, it was the following day, when Mum's room took on a joyful party atmosphere. The dark storm clouds of rage were gone. As luck would have it I didn't have to work. Mum's sister Noreen arrived from the country. My son, Jordie, managed to get a last-minute flight from America and arrived that morning and sat in Mum's room playing guitar and singing songs all day. Relatives came and went—grandchildren, siblings, nieces, nephews, cousins, in-laws—and we all laughed a lot.

COMEDY AND DEATH

Noreen told us about the time 'Marg and I were in the city—it was during the war—and we were on our way to a dance. We were crossing over Swanston Street and blow me down if Marg didn't get hit by a hearse. She didn't let that stop her, though—there was no way she was going to miss that dance, so she just brushed herself off and away we went. Gawd, Marg loved to dance. There was that time in Tat, one night, I've never forgotten it. Your mother had a brand-new white fur coat. She'd saved all year for it. She loved it. It was beautiful too, real soft white fur. Anyway, so she goes to this dance, puts her coat in the cloakroom, comes back at the end of the night and it's gone—in its place a tatty, dirty, thin, old white fur coat. It broke your mother's heart. But geez, we had some fun, cos of course we used to sleep in the same bed for years in Tat, in the old sleep-out in the backyard. We had Cocky the cockatoo in the cage right behind us, and, poor Marg, she'd go out on a date and come home late, and she'd be trying to sneak in, and Cocky would be screaming, "Hello Marg! Hello Marg! Hello Marg!" and Marg would be saying, "Sh! Shut up, Cocky," but he'd just yell even louder, "SCRATCH COCKY, MARG!" Oh Gawd, we'd laugh. And you know Jimmy, well, after we started going out together, he used to sneak into the sleep-out and lie down between Marg and me on that bed, and fall asleep …'

'I bet he did, Noreen!'

'No, it's true. He did! As soon as his head hit the pillow, *bang*, his eyes would be closed and he'd be out like a light, for hours. That's truck drivers for you. Oh gee, we had some laughs.'

Although Mum was not conscious I could tell she was happy and calm, relieved to have her sister there. At 5 pm

Noreen kissed my mother goodbye, held her hand, and said, 'Rightio then, see you next time.'

At 2.58 am the next morning, my mother died. My sister, my niece, John and I were with her. She died peacefully.

Three hours later John drove me to the *Winners and Losers* set. It was the day of the big wedding scene. It was bizarre—there I was, dancing the macarena in the Rippon Lea ballroom with my onscreen husband, played by Francis Greenslade, appearing to have the time of my life, when only a few hours earlier I had held my mother's hand as she passed from this world.

I told the producers and Francis, but no-one else, what had taken place that morning. At one point one of the cast took aside the assistant director and reported a 'weird extra who seems to be harassing Denise. Every time we stop filming he goes and sits with her.' The 'weird extra' was John. He had come with me to offer his emotional support, and whenever the cameras stopped rolling, he was helping me organise Mum's funeral.

The producers kindly found a body double for me so I could leave the filming early. She slipped into my costume and shoes, and wore a blonde wig that was fashioned to be similar to my hair. From the back she was identical to me—hence the psychological trauma for cast members when they called out, 'Hey, Denise …' and a twenty-five-year-old woman with a teeny, tiny pixie face they'd never seen before turned around to answer them.

My sister and I were sitting at the table in my kitchen. Her job was to write a eulogy covering all milestones: where Mum was born, where she grew up, when she married, and so on. I was working on a separate eulogy, focussing on funny stories.

Julie looked up from her note making. 'What will I say about Mum's parents?'

'I guess just say the truth: Margaret Scott, daughter of May …'

'Do you think? I mean, does everyone know that?'

'I think so. Anyway, too bad if they don't. It's the truth.'

'Yeah, but would Mum want us to say it? There might be someone there who gets upset, and Mum would hate that.'

'I don't want anyone to be upset, either, but Mum was May's daughter. What else can we say?'

'So should I name all her siblings?'

'Yes. Let's just do it.'

Writing a eulogy for our mother wasn't easy, because since Dad's death all those years ago it seemed not much had happened that we could tell stories about—at least, not joyful stories. So Julie and I found ourselves writing about the old days—the war, Dad's clown costume, their mutual love of dancing. I finished with the story about the elephant pulling us out of the bog.

As unresolved about God's existence as I was, I chose to believe that in the afterlife Mum and Dad would be reunited. It made me feel happy, picturing the smile returning to my mother's face.

The funeral was a jolly affair.

John played the ukulele and we had a singalong. Jordie played the guitar and sang 'Somewhere over the rainbow'.

Bonnie read a poem.

My sister's children did readings and showed photos of Mum.

Julie and I read our eulogies.

At the graveside, Julie and I watched our mother's coffin being lowered into the ground. Everyone else stood at a respectful distance behind us.

Suddenly, I became aware of someone squeezing between my sister and me. I turned my head and saw a young man, no more than fourteen years of age, and I thought to myself, Who the hell is this? before I recalled that of course he was my cousin's son.

Just as Mum's coffin came to rest at the bottom of the grave—an intensely poignant moment—this young man leant towards me and said, 'So, Denise, got any tips for getting started in comedy?'

I looked at him in shock and then said, 'Actually, I do. Timing. It's all about timing.'

Marg Scott (left) Matron Barnes (middle) and Mrs Ellis (also a nurse) off to the Oaks Day races, mid 1960s—our house was the one behind them, without the trees

Acknowledgements

Big thanks:
    To Fran Berry, from Hardie Grant, for once more publishing me and also for completely ignoring me whenever I rang, emailed or appeared in her office declaring: 'You can have the advance back, I can't write this book.'

To Rose Michael, editor extraordinaire and supreme queen of tact who, after wading through my first draft (or, as I liked to call it, my pile of vomit), declared: 'Well, there's a book in there.' I was, of course, mystified and asked: 'Where?' Without batting an eyelid Rose calmly repeated: 'It's in there.' When I asked once more, this time with a high-pitched, squeaky voice, indicating extreme stress: 'But where in there?' Rose replied: 'You'll find it.' At the time I didn't believe her but she was right, for better or worse, I did find a book, 'in there'. So thank you, Rose, not only for your mighty editing prowess, but your incredible support.

To Penny Mansley, another editor extraordinaire! Penny was quite literally dynamite, so much so that at one point, as her edits, suggestions and questions kept popping up, day and night, non-stop, in my inbox, I did wonder if she was on some kind of Red Bull and speed cocktail mix. Apparently not, it seems she's just driven and brilliant at her job.

To Stu and Gideon who were there on the day of my roadside epiphany and who kindly never released the photos.

To Susan Provan and her team for creating the Melbourne International Comedy Festival Roadshow—it really does change lives.

To Judith Lucy. Throughout this whole process she has been there for me. The fact that she was also writing her second memoir at the same time meant we could get together, drink a glass of wine (not easy to do when curled in the foetal position, I found one of those bendy straws useful), and talk through our anxieties and self-doubts. I am blessed to have her as a friend and work colleague.

To my gorgeous sister Julie Scott. Without her support I simply would not have been able to write this book. And a big thank you to my Aunty Noreen who is so funny and such good company and was always such a wonderful, loyal and loving sister to my mother Marg.

To both my parents, Marg and Russ, and their extended families—the Scott's and the Young's—I give thanks for being part of such a wonderful and fascinating clan.

To my good friend Fran Jenkins, who is like a sister to me, for all the encouragement she gave me during the writing of *The Tour*. And thanks also to author Kirsty Murray, whose helpful advice and support arrived at a point in time when I so desperately needed it.

To all at Token, especially Kevin, Dioni and Zoe for your

tireless, ongoing support and for just making so much exciting stuff happen in my work life!

To Jordie and Bonnie Lane who continue to amaze and inspire me.

And finally, to John Lane. Always there and willing to listen, to give me feedback, gee me up, put a positive spin on things and who, without doubt, ensures my life is never ordinary.

Author's note

Although all the people and events in this book are very much real, on the odd occasion I have changed people's names in order to protect the innocent, and the guilty, and ultimately myself.